DEPRESSION MODERN

Frontispiece: Radio City Music Hall, New York City, 1933.

MARTIN GREIF

DEPRESSION MODERN
THE THIRTIES STYLE IN AMERICA

UNIVERSE · BOOKS · NEW · YORK

Published in the United States of America in 1975
by Universe Books
381 Park Avenue South
New York, N.Y. 10016

© 1975 by Martin Greif
Second printing, 1977

Library of Congress Catalog Card Number: 75-11140
Cloth edition: ISBN 0-87663-257-6
Paperback edition: ISBN 0-87663-925-2

Printed in the United States of America

Designed by Robert Reed

IN MEMORY OF
J. B. L. ANDRADA
1929—1975

This one's for you, Joe.

CONTENTS

¶

ACKNOWLEDGMENTS

The idea for this book is Larry Grow's. Having heard me talk about the 1930s on and off for the past ten years, he suggested that I stop talking and start writing. For his impatience, good counsel, and friendship, I am grateful.

For reasons that go far beyond the compilation of this book, I am indebted to Donald Deskey, Wallace K. Harrison, George Fred Keck, Raymond Loewy, Edward Durell Stone, and Russel Wright, young men all during the Great Depression who have taught me, among other things, that Browning knew what he was talking about when he wrote the opening lines of *Rabbi Ben Ezra*. After coming to know Donald Deskey and Russel Wright in particular, I doubt that I will ever again fear old age.

The photographer Robert Damora, the designer John D. Gerald, and the architects W. E. Bentzinger, John A. Holabird, Jr., Samuel E. Homsey, Wesley V. Pipher, and T. Trip Russell have all responded generously to requests for information about design during the Great Depression.

Kay Sakier has graciously shared with me her memories of the 1930s as has Lillian Kiesler, artist and friend, whose dedication to the genius of her late husband, Frederick Kiesler, is the stuff of fine poetry and even greater love.

Of the many people who have supplied me with rare archival material for this book, several have been unstinting and tireless in their energies and detective work. Of these, H. E. B. Anderson, Director of Information of The Austin Company, Cleveland, Ohio, emerged from dank storage basements, dust-covered and disheveled, more than once in my behalf, and Diane Thaler, secretary to Raymond Loewy, mixed efficiency with wondrously earthly humor in assisting me through ten years of Mr. Loewy's files. William B. May, Jr., arranged a guided tour through one of his properties so that I could have a first-hand architectural understanding of a 1930s apartment house, from boiler room to penthouse. Peggy S. Huffman of the Hedrich-Blessing Studio, Chicago, Illinois, has come up with solutions to every problem sent her, even though the clues were often as slender as a thread. I acknowledge, too, the extraordinary cooperation of Robert P. Scott, Manager, Advertising and Public Relations, Burroughs Corporation, Business Forms and Supplies Group, Rochester, New York; Alan K. Lathrop, Curator, Northwest Architectural Archives, Minneapolis, Minnesota; Isobel C. Lee, Vice President, Steuben Glass, New York City; and Nicholas Polites, Walter Dorwin Teague Associates, Inc., New York City.

I am grateful, also, for the assistance of Douglas Hahn, B. Altman & Co., New York City; Byron S. Campbell, Aluminum Company of America, Pittsburgh, Pennsylvania; Clara H. Noack, County Clerk, Alpena County, Michigan; Alvin F. Gunther, Gibbons—Hollyday & Ives, Inc., New York City; Eileen Wosick, Ogden & Company, Milwaukee, Wisconsin; Richard B. Sinclair, Armstrong Cork Company, Lancaster, Pennsylvania; Robbie Y. Kestner, The Wm. H. Block Co., Indianapolis, Indiana; Robert C. Reese, Campana Corporation, Batavia, Illinois; Annchen T. Swanson, The Chase Manhattan Bank, N.A., New York City; Wilbur George Kurtz, Jr., The Coca-Cola Company, Atlanta, Georgia; Peggy James, Colorado Springs Fine Arts Center, Colorado Springs, Colorado.

Also Bob Fuller, CBS Radio, New York City; Dixie Lee Stringer, Columbia Public Schools, Columbia, Mississippi; L. Henry Liese, Cranbrook Educational Community, Bloomfield Hills, Michigan; Janice C. Greer, Dictaphone Corporation, Rye, New York; Lucille Wolz, County Clerk, Ector County, Texas; Edward Markey, Electrolux Corporation, Stamford, Connecticut; Ann Oliva, The Emporium, San Francisco, California; Helen E. Noah, First Federal Savings and Loan Association of New York, Bronxville, New York; Michael C. Contezac, U.S. Department of Agriculture Forest Service, Madison, Wisconsin; Elizabeth D. Marshall, The Great Atlantic & Pacific Tea Company, Inc., Montvale, New Jersey; Eleanor Adams, Halle's, Cleveland, Ohio.

Also David M. Nellis, The Hecht Co., Washington, D.C.; J. D. Atkins, Houston First Savings Association, Houston, Texas; A. L. McCormick, Principal, Edward L. Bailey Junior High School, Jackson, Mississippi; Eunice McMurtry, Johnson & Johnson, New Brunswick, New Jersey; Neal J. Seiser, S. C. Johnson & Son, Inc., Racine, Wisconsin; Warren R. Erickson, The Meyercord Co., Chicago, Illinois; E. H. Daws, U.S. Postal Service, Miami, Florida; Anne Read, Herman Miller, Inc., Zeeland, Michigan.

Also Charlotte La Rue, Museum of the City of New York; M. L. Melville, NCR Corporation, Dayton, Ohio; Frank P. Howard, Oregon State Highway Division, Salem, Oregon; Ann Whyte, Pan American World Airways, Inc., New York City; Jack Shuba, Pennzoil Company, Los Angeles, California; C. E. Weber, Precision Spring Corporation, Detroit, Michigan; Frida Schubert, RCA, New York City; H. T. S. Heckman, Republic Steel Corporation, Cleveland, Ohio; Chris Sanson, *The Shreveport Times,* Shreveport, Louisiana; John W. Hubbell, Simmons Company, New York City; Kathy Leonard, Southern California Gas Company, Los Angeles, California.

Also M. Forster, Star Electrical Supply Co., Newark, New Jersey; Lillian Owens, Time Inc. Archives, New York City; David J. Gizer, Trans-Lux, New York City; George Schoepfer, Triborough Bridge and Tunnel Authority, New York City; Jean C. Burnett, Wadsworth Atheneum, Hartford, Connecticut; R. H. Vogt, Wear-Ever Aluminum Inc., Chillicothe, Ohio; and J. R. van Leuwen, F. W. Woolworth Co., New York City.

Many people searched through musty files and corporate archives to supply me with information and photographs which, for lack of space, have not been included in this book. I am pleased, therefore, to record my debt to Edward A. Metzger, Borchard Management Corporation, New York City; Bev Eastman, Eastman's Gaslight Room, Detroit, Michigan; Leo DeFer, Boulder Valley Public Schools, Boulder, Colorado; Lee L. Burtis, California Historical Society, San Francisco, California; Ann Tellman, Cannon Mills, Inc., New York City; Peg Dann, The Cincinnati Historical Society; Joan Levers, The Children's Hospital, Denver, Colorado; Otto W. Hilbert, Corning Glass Works, Corning, New York.

Also Robert F. English, Cutler Mail Chute Division, Cutler-Federal, Inc., Eaton Park, Florida; Albert C. Kelley, Medical Products Division, The De Vilbiss Company, Somerset, Pennsylvania; Lu Ann Porter, Dunbar Furniture Division, General Interiors Corporation, Berne, Indiana; David Hartley, *The Herald Statesman,* Yonkers, New York; Kenneth L. Bowers, Hershey Foods Corporation, Hershey, Pennsylvania; Nancy Burt, Hollywood High School, Hollywood, California; Augustin S. Hardart, Jr., The Horn & Hardart Company, New York City; E. P. Hogan, International Silver Company, Meriden, Connecticut; H. Ray Goldwire, Kimble Division, Owens-Illinois, Inc., Vineland, New Jersey; Arthur Riback, National Restaurants, Inc., New York City.

Also Grace Teed Kent, Longchamps Restaurants, New York City; Robert A. Mann, The B. Manischewitz Company, Newark, New Jersey; K. D. Magill, The Mennen Company, Morristown, New Jersey; Martin H. Feinman, Modernage Furniture, Miami, Florida; A. J. Swartz, Modine Manufacturing Co., Racine, Wisconsin; John F. Majeski, *The Music Trades,* Englewood, New Jersey; Frank Lloyd, The Philadelphia Art Alliance; Robert E. Buckley, Pittsburgh Corning Corporation; Ross R. Fernow, Glass Advertising & Promotion, PPG Industries, Pittsburgh, Pennsylvania; William J. Bassett, *The Daily Item,* Port Chester, New York; Lloyd B. Plummer, San Diego Federal Savings and Loan Association; Marsha Lane, Schenley Affiliated Brands Corp., New York City; Mayor Betty Davis, City of South Haven, Michigan; Dan P. Thornton, Spreckels Sugar Division, Amstar Corporation, San Francisco, California; Phyllis McCullough, Thonet Industries, Inc., York, Pennsylvania; Willis Ranney, United Airlines, Chicago, Illinois; Robert L. Mason, U.S. National Bank of Oregon, Klamath Falls, Oregon; Donn Dutcher, Western Union Telegraph Co., Mahwah, New Jersey; and Dorothy B. Strayer, The White Plains Hospital, White Plains, New York.

The furniture of Frederick Kiesler pictured in this book is, with two exceptions, from the collection of Martha Bartos and was originally designed for Mr. and Mrs. Charles Mergentime. Of the remaining two pieces, the aluminum kidney-shaped tables are from the collection of Mr. and Mrs. Donald Grossman, and the aluminum coffee table is shown in an original photograph taken in 1936. I am grateful to the owners of these important Kiesler pieces for permission to reproduce them in these pages.

In the compilation and writing of this book I have been encouraged by my friends Clive Driver, David Lindstrom, and, especially, Helen Iranyi, all of whom have had to put up with a great deal of talk about the 1930s. Finally, I have been fortunate in my editor, Lou Barron, without whose thoughtful advice and gentlemanly kindness *Depression Modern* would have been an entirely different book.

PREFACE

Photos in an album, yellowed, faded, worn. Moments frozen in memory worlds ago, but recorded only forty years ago in time. Fragments distant, but startlingly familiar.

My mother at twenty, handsome and slender, her evening dress shaped to her figure, bias-cut and backless, clinging and revealing, soft and flattering. My father at twenty-six, proudly showing off his first-born on a spring morning in 1933, an uncle (his eye to the camera) reflected carelessly in the curved, steel-rimmed window of the local bakery. My elder brother at four, at play in the courtyard of a new apartment house with round-cornered casements, his tricycle and the scooter of a small friend streamlined to resemble the latest Chrysler "Airflow" motor car. A neighbor, looking older than her twenty-one years, her small felt hat worn rakishly to one side and revealing waved hair set close to the head, a sleek figure in black crêpe de Chine jacket and white jabot, posed before the gleaming glass block and Vitrolite façade of Ann's Beauty Salon. A birthday party in the late 1930s for a five-year-old, the neighborhood children (four of whom, round-faced and banana-curled, are named Shirley) crowded expectantly around the oblong blonde-wood dining table, its matching, gift-laden sideboard, gracefully rounded, smooth, and mass-produced without ornament, set beneath a frameless, circular, peach-tinted mirror. A snapshot of an infant in the summer of 1939, the author at fourteen months, asleep in a polished-enamel perambulator, maroon in color, a horizontal band of three slender steel stripes across its side, a baby carriage with lines like the family's Pontiac, a line that starts with a parabolic curve and ends in a long backward sweep, the same line recurring in photograph after photograph, in clothing and furniture, in automobile and storefront—the fundamental line of an age. And then—seen against the Trylon and Perisphere, the vast white curves of the New York World's Fair—my parents, young and American, their backs turned to events in Europe, their eyes widened and corrupted by the modern wonders of "The World of Tomorrow," a glass and steel and streamlined phoenix emerging triumphant from the devastation of the Great Depression.

Each succeeding generation is false to its predecessor in reconstructing and interpreting the events of the past, in selecting and stressing the details that conform to its notion of an age recently become history, in sentimentalizing or libeling the days and years of its elders. And—in punishing its parents by distorting their era, their time in the sun—my generation is no different from any other.

Perhaps no American period in memory has been so falsified and fictionalized as that of the 1930s. TV shows are set in the period for no apparent reason. Articles on this or that aspect of it appear daily in newspapers and in popular magazines. Its entertainers and celebrities—many second-rate and justly anonymous to two generations—are rediscovered and packaged as momentary, but passing, fancies. Its styles and fashions are ransacked and adapted and briefly revived by the chic and by the middle-class young. Inevitably, Hollywood—most responsible for our ''first-hand'' vision of the '30s as we view old films on television—distorts it still further by creating it anew as plastic fodder for today's motion pictures. This time, however, the shadow is twice removed from the substance (the Dream Factory's original vision of itself forty years ago being once removed from reality), and reflects, of economic necessity, the present obsession with raw sex and violence, eternal concerns treated quite differently during the Great Depression. The sycophantic imitations of Bogdanovich, the very face and voice of Streisand, the make-up of Dunaway, the pin-striped suits of Redford and Newman are totally false to the 1930s—hard-edged vulgarizations of its soft-edged sophistication and calculating condescensions to its naïve innocence.

The Hollywood of the '70s, aware of the superficial parallels between the two decades, grinds out ''period'' fantasies, set gratuitously in a mythologized Depression, whether the time is integral to the plot or not. But the characters are all either Steinbeck-poor or Brenda Frazier-rich. And the clothes are wrong, the hairdos oddly contemporary, the music ludicrously anachronistic—either Scott Joplin (then passé and at least twenty years ignored and forgotten) or the clipped rhythms of a Cole Porter or a Harry Warren, muted, modernized, and Muzak'd. Whether the date portrayed is 1931 or 1938, the settings are alive, conspicuously, with Art Deco—all zigzags and neo-Cubist designs, ersatz Lalique, and porcelain statuettes of flappers in cloche hats—the Jazz Age mysteriously set down, as if by some strange time machine, in the midst of the Great Depression. But for those in the audience who might be watching, only the Pierce-Arrows, the Hupmobiles and Packards are right, a concession not so much to accuracy as to the only shared history left us: the history of America's veneration of the automobile.

The current vogue for things bizarre and, particularly, for the extravagant, the exotic, and the erotic, has crescendoed through the 1960s into the present decade. It explains, perhaps, the enormous popularity of Art Deco today and why, of all things associated with the '20s and '30s, Art Deco has most captured the imaginations of the gay set, the decorators, the admen, and other trend-setters —and, ultimately, the fancies of the young, the kitsch collectors, the falsely sophisticated, and most other trend-followers.

At its best (and it was frequently superb), Art Deco was a style consummately Parisian, "smart" rather than pretty, embraced not by the French avant-garde, not by the conservative old-rich, but by those who liked to think of themselves as tastemakers: couturières, decorators, theatrical designers, and others catering to the *haut monde*. As such, Deco was of passing importance, a snobbish badge of exclusivity adopted by the few and known to still fewer, a style characterized by its use of luxurious materials: Macassar ebony in furniture, shagreen and ivory as trim, the finest leather, lacquer, and enamel that money could buy.

In its self-indulgent pursuit of exclusivity and luxury, it appealed to those whose lives were devoted to modishness, a thing to be ridiculed in the pages of Evelyn Waugh once it traveled across the Channel, and a fashion totally Americanized (and bastardized) after it crossed the Atlantic to the land of mass production. And, as we shall see, it was obsessively romantic and backward-looking, finding inspiration in the ornate past, the very antithesis of the modern and its radical emphasis on functional simplicity. As the plaything of the fashionable, the palliative of the vain, Art Deco's orchidaceous flowering in the '20s was to be withered, ultimately, by the cold winds of the Depressed '30s. And once it sacrificed its urbane exclusivity on the mechanized altar of the American assembly line, it lost its very *raison d'être*.

Deco in America enjoyed a short-lived vogue as superficially applied decoration on lipstick holders, cigarette cases, compacts, and the like. But there is no Art Deco to be found in my family album. Nor is there any in the albums of anyone else I know. I can find no ebony furniture, no stylized African sculpture or cubistic decoration in these photographs, even though my parents and their contemporaries did visit the dazzling interiors of Radio City Music Hall more than once in the decade, realizing, of course, that movie palaces and hotel lobbies were to be looked at and not lived in. There is, in fact, little of Deco, authentic or vulgarized, to be found in contemporary American magazines, either. *The Smart Set,* apparently, was not smart enough for it. *Fortune* was too conservative. *The New Yorker* (ridiculing most things "modern") restricted it to occasional appearances in jewelry advertisements. *Time* (frozen in its original 1923 format) ignored it, and *Life* was born too late for it. Although there are in the pages of these magazines glimpses of spoutless teapots with lids dizzily askew, of square Depression-glass dinnerware, or of zigzagging, geometric dress clips, asymmetric perfume bottles, and Jazz Age display type, these are far outnumbered by objects, layouts, and type faces that are simply curved, eloquently understated, elegantly unornamented. What impresses one most, in fact, in thumbing through magazines of the '30s, is clarity of line, simplicity, and directness—graphic precision largely free of hokey "trendiness," a much more recent journalistic invention.

And yet the belief persists today that Art Deco and the decade of the '30s are somehow synonymous, a popular misconception spread almost universally by contemporary pop-culturists and the advertising media, aped slavishly by fashionable magazines and the feature pages of our daily newspapers, and embraced enthusiastically, but ignorantly, by the young, the lazy, the unthinking, and those whose only view of the period is through the prismatic lens of Hollywood. When an Art Deco "festival" can be held annually at Radio City Music Hall, its once-elegant foyer and lounges polluted by dealers hawking to the multitudes everything from World War I song sheets to World War II platform shoes, all masquerading as gen-u-ine "Art Deco"; when *The New York Times* can report this phenomenon *uncritically* as a page-one event; when a slick magazine can include in its photographic gallery of Art Deco buildings masterpieces of the International Style; when an otherwise intelligent film critic can praise the brilliant modern design and almost-Bauhaus trappings of *Things to Come* (1936) as "vintage Art Deco"; when a popular TV talk-show emcee can babble knowingly about "Art Deco of the *1940s*," meaning snoods and veils and padded shoulder-pads—something has gone wrong with our critical vocabulary, if not our critical acumen. These people are all like the goose in the barnyard, honking at the rising sun, lacking memories and foresight. It is as if yesterday never happened and tomorrow will never come, as if everything from the recent past were one and the same, as if Bette Midler had invented the Wurlitzer jukebox.

It is time, I think, to have another look.

_____

_____

_____

This book does not pretend to be a scholarly *dissertation d'un auteur*. It is, rather, an informal and informed appreciation of a period I happen to like. Although it is carefully and, I hope, accurately researched, it is essentially a personal document, an attempt, largely visual, to rescue the '30s—or one particular aspect of it—from those who, in their uncritical enthusiasm and perverse love for the decade, have distorted, suffocated, and nearly killed it.

As such, the book has two purposes. Its minor aim is to correct a misconception, that Art Deco was the predominant style of the 1930s—a misconception which obscures the essentially modern spirit of the time. On the contrary, the major American designers of the Great Depression hated Deco (which they considered "the modern deprived of its manhood") and despised its effete luxuriousness, adjudging its romantic backsliding a betrayal and perversion of modernism. What they created, largely in reaction against Deco, was a new machine art: honest, simple, and functionally expressive—values basic alike to the house, the school, the streamlined train, the cigarette lighter, the toaster, the saucepan, or the grand piano as these emerged from the designer's studio. What they created they called the "Modern," a term (to my eye, at any rate) still visually acceptable, but chronologically imperfect. I have chosen instead to call it "Depression Modern," suggesting both its time and its place: America in the 1930s.

The second aim of this book, its fundamental purpose, is to define and illustrate Depression Modern as the primary style of the decade, a design revolution which, in my opinion, was the turning point of modernism in America. By focusing on the period between two great expositions—Chicago's Century of Progress (1933–34) and the New York World's Fair (1939–40)—it shows that a relatively small group of young, brilliant, energetic designers of the 1930s attempted to create, perhaps for the first time, a national style that was uniquely American, despite its European borrowings—a style basically the same in New York, Mississippi, Arizona, Montana, Minnesota, or California. So revolutionary was this style, in fact, so all-pervasive, that in a period of only half a decade it changed the shape of virtually everything in the American home, including, finally, the home itself. So total was its success, so complete its acceptance (we live surrounded by its offspring today), that its origins in the 1930s and its innovative creators, if not completely forgotten, are now simply taken for granted. Thus does popular history reward the victors.

Depression Modern: The Thirties Style in America, by defining a neglected but important contribution to design, and especially through the pictorial recreation of that style in its album of contemporary photographs, intends to set the record straight.

As the decade began: the way things looked *before* Depression Modern.

DEPRESSION MODERN
AN APPRECIATION

"*Beauty, like truth, is never so glorious
as when it goes the plainest.*"
—Laurence Sterne

"*We should be more efficient, Sir, if less decorated.*"
—a Persian general to his emperor, fifth century B.C.

1

On a wintry Friday night in 1938, a throng of theatergoers, several primping in their evening clothes as they emerge from the blasts of a February wind, jostle their way through a fashionable crowd in the lobby of a New York playhouse. From the close perfumed warmth of the foyer, those nearest the chrome and glass doors can witness the frenetic bustle of the theater district in the hectic minutes before an 8:30 curtain. Outside, through frosty panes, moves a procession of the modern, a kaleidoscope of the mechanical, the metallic din of klaxons muted only by the icy wind.

Packard limousines, sleek and black, the iridescent neon of Broadway reflected in their slanted rear windows, disgorge the rich and privileged, their liveried drivers banished until the play's final act to coffee over red Micarta tables at the 42nd Street Cafeteria. In herds of twos and threes, fat arch-backed Yellow Cabs issue passengers picked up a quarter-hour earlier under the canopies and curved marquees of the Century, the Majestic, the Eldorado, and other smart apartment buildings on Central Park West. Suburban matrons, supping in town, their brightly lipsticked mouths freshened with after-dinner mints, dart between the cabs from the gleaming Thermolux vestibule of a wine-colored Long-champs across the street. Their unmarried daughters, playing at being career girls in the months before fashionable June weddings, leave unwashed china in apartment kitchenettes, silk stockings thrown hastily over the iron railings of dropped living rooms. Others, with their beaus, pass through leather-quilted doors pierced with chrome-ringed portholes, abandoning cups of steaming chocolate at the glass-brick fountain of the Taft Hotel. Young couples, their chesterfields and Persian lambs braced to the wind, hurry crosstown from streamlined Fifth Avenue buses, passing on their way the revolving doors and circular change booths of Automats and the ghostly blue mirrors of cheap chop suey joints, as the Sixth Avenue El rumbles overhead.

Suffusing all are the flashing lights of New York's Broadway in the late 1930s—urban America encircled, as it were, by a mechanical nimbus: the hissing and puffing A&P coffeepot sign. Adjacent, above a gaudy movie-vaudeville house, illuminated by a thousand bulbs, an enormous billboard, advertising MGM's *Test Pilot,* exploits the box-office popularity of Clark Gable and Myrna Loy— and the public's love affair with swift and shiny airplanes. Across the wide avenue at the Paramount, another blinking sign entices the radio fan to *The Big Broadcast of 1938,* with Fields and Hope and Flagstad and a dozen top stars of the airwaves aboard a dazzlingly white luxury liner. At Roseland, a few blocks uptown, a band breaking into swing announces the Lambeth Walk and the Big Apple, while a monocled Mr. Peanut, squinting grotesquely in red neon, is reflected in a passing Times Square trolley. Dominant over the east wall of the urban ravine, an enormous eleven-fished aquarium, advertising chewing gum, starts to flicker and sparkle, its colossal guppies blowing green and yellow neon bubbles. A photo-electric animated cartoon tells how to be a success at love, offering the example of a square-headed hero who smokes Old Golds. Beyond, a resplendent orange spurts radiance like a sun, an equally garish lemon looming higher than the orange. Both shimmer high above a theater showing the latest chapter of *The March of Time:* "Inside Nazi Germany."

Broadway on the night of February 4, 1938. The premiere performance of Thornton Wilder's *Our Town*—a play, ironically, that celebrates the timeless excitement of the ordinary.

In setting forth his story of the loves, deaths, and the patterns of everyday life in a small New England village, Thornton Wilder placed *Our Town* in the recent past: Grover's Corners, New Hampshire, in the year 1901, a time within living memory of many, if not most, of his audience. Presented on a stage bare of scenery, and reflecting both the sophisticated stripped-down art of the late 1930s and the innocent period of its setting, *Our Town* evoked the simple pleasures of a day just moments in time before the clamor of automobile traffic and the roar of whirling airplane propellers: a day, only thirty-seven years before, in which Editor Webb's wife baked pies in the oven of a wood-burning castiron range and Grover's Corners' only doctor made his rounds in a horse-drawn phaeton; a time in which George and Emily's young love blossomed over strawberry phosphates at the marble counter of the local drugstore.

The audience of *Our Town,* heirs of the 19th century, had lived with wide-eyed amazement through more than three decades of almost miraculous industrial growth, through a period of inventive progress intensified by a great war abroad. It had enjoyed (and was beginning to take for granted) the widespread mechanical wonders of the telephone and the radio, of talking pictures and the automobile, of speeding stainless-steel Burlington Zephyrs and transcontinental Flying Clippers. To this audience, the dimly familiar but alien world of Grover's Corners at the start of the century might never have existed. To this Depression audience, the world of 1901—with its buggies and wooden washtubs, its hot-water bottles and mustard plasters, its horsehair cushions and velvet hair ribbons —might just as well have occurred a thousand years ago on an uncharted island or on a distant planet. So far had America progressed in only thirty-seven years.

Thornton Wilder's *Our Town* stands midway between the opening years of the century's first and final quarters: midway between our generation of the 1970s and George and Emily's at the beginning of the 20th century. Exactly thirty-seven years separate its first performance in 1938 from the events in 1901 within the play itself. Exactly the same number of years separate its premiere from the present day. But if its first-night audience, repressing memories almost four decades distant, gazed as foreigners on the landscape of its youth, scarcely recognizing an earlier world portrayed so starkly that February night thirty-seven years ago, then we today look back with relative ease to a period equidistantly removed from us in time, but far less strange. We look back with an altogether different feeling of surprise at the physical world of 1938.

Look. The cabs, the cars, the planes, the buses, the restaurants, the lights, the bustle, the din are with us still. Nothing much has changed.

In 1934 Raymond Loewy executed a famous series of "evolution charts," illustrating the tendency toward simplification and sheerness in everything from automobiles, airplanes, and railroad trains to glassware and women's fashions. Many of the following charts also illustrate the origins of streamlining and of the new horizontality.

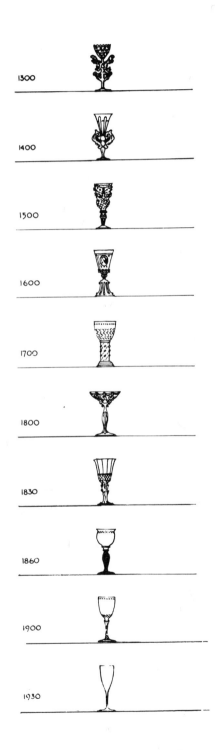

1300
1400
1500
1600
1700
1800
1830
1860
1900
1930

In 1938, the average American wife, homebound and dependent, listened to Kate Smith or Bing Crosby or Whispering Jack Smith while doing her daily housework. Her kitchen companion, if she were lucky or if her husband were working regularly, was a new table-model radio, placed securely atop the mechanical refrigerator, beneath the chrome and enamel electric wall clock and away from the exploring hands of little children. More frequently, however, in homes with only one radio, the living room console was turned up so that the housewife could enjoy *Aunt Jenny* while doing the wash in the family Toperator or Maytag or Bendix, or could listen to *Joyce Jordan, Girl Intern* while vacuuming the carpet with upright Kwik-Kleen or streamlined Electrolux. On the kitchen table, then as now, a two-slice automatic toaster. On the white square stove, its corners gently rounded, aluminum or stainless cookware with Bakelite handles. In the pantry or cabinet, in direct proportion to the family income, an assortment of electric appliances from waffle irons and coffeepots to clothes irons and broilers, from oscillating fans and mixers to heating pads and sun lamps. And in the kitchens of the affluent: garbage disposals and automatic dishwashers, their ubiquity halted only by the oncoming clouds of a world at war.

One could catalogue endlessly the points of correspondence between the physical worlds of 1938 and today, between its mundane possessions and ours, between its mechanical triumphs and ours: glass walled, air-conditioned office towers and apartment buildings, television (both black-and-white and color), frozen foods, solar-heated homes, and on and on and on. All were demonstrably practical and commercially viable thirty-seven years ago, even if their widespread development was interrupted for almost a decade by the economies of war and by the necessary reconstruction of Europe.

But if we can so readily find in 1938 a mechanical world undreamed of in the America of *Our Town*, if we can easily recognize the functional similarities between the objects of 1938 and of today, how even more astonishing are the characteristic shapes of these objects, so familiar to us, so similar to those of our day, and so dramatically different from those of the previous decade of the '20s.

What is it, exactly, about the "shape of the '30s," and about the last half of the decade in particular, that so suggests modernity? What is it that makes an Eleanor Powell, tapping however ridiculously atop a sleek white battleship in 1936, so much more modern-looking than a Ruby Keeler, tapping just as ridiculously three years earlier aboard a dumpy sleeper shuffling off to Buffalo?

We needn't look to the rich or glamorous to discover just how modern the '30s were. Commonplaces will do, or even objects from Sears, Roebuck catalogues: bathroom scales or clocks or table lamps or basement burners. We need look no further, actually, than within the kitchen of Andy Hardy's mother, within the scrubbed and gingham pantry of Louis B. Mayer's idealized Middle America, to understand what it is that makes the decade seem so peculiarly contemporary. Mickey Rooney's 1938 screen-mother baked cookies in a kitchen very much like the kitchens of today, but vastly different from those of his Mickey McGuire days of the late '20s, a day in which a kitchen was a dreary affair furnished with a long-legged stove, a rickety china cupboard, and an enamel worktable set halfway across the room from a sink and washtub, standing stark and bare-limbed with plumbing rusting and exposed.

Although Judge Hardy, if he ever existed, exists no more, the 1938 kitchen of his wife still does. And it reflects in the material world, in the world of objects and of things, a revolution that occurred in the 1930s—a revolution in design and in the shape of things as dynamic as any that occurred in contemporary social thought: a movement from the vertical to the horizontal, from the straight line to the curve—both preferred, in their purest employment, for functional ends, and in their basest use, for the value of a marketable appearance.

Mrs. Hardy's stove, a gracefully rounded white square, set flush between glistening cabinet-counters and adjacent to a Monel metal sink, is as a building block in a functional and expressive unit of blocks arranged contiguously around the room. It is essentially an American design: the work of Norman Bel Geddes as filtered down through the popularized advertisements of Westinghouse and General Electric and Armstrong Floors and other corporations appealing to the American consumer. Mrs. Hardy's kitchen, its horizontal units of white blocks all exactly the same height and repeated in the long row of wall cabinets above, is identical to the one in which Penny Singleton, masquerading as Chic Young's Blondie, prepares dinner for Dagwood and Baby Dumpling, or in which Spring Byington as Mrs. Jones, the all-American Depression housewife, solves the pressing problems of her dim-witted husband. With its man-sized refrigerator and Formica cabinet tops, its Venetian blinds and inlaid linoleum floor, this modular kitchen is undoubtedly the most modern room in the 1938 house. It is, fundamentally, and with no substantial changes, the room in which we still prepare our meals today.

If the kitchen of 1938, glistening and utilitarian, bears little resemblance to that of just a few years earlier—say, to the kitchen of 1929—then the same dissimilarity is equally true of the objects found within both rooms. An electric fan, no longer standing at attention—as did its '20s predecessor—arches gracefully, its form resembling, consciously, that of an airplane, ovoid and gliding. A toaster, all polished chrome and curved, is longer and lower than the '20s model. It bears the same relationship to its earlier, taller, more vertical forebear as does the long, curved profile of the Broadway Limited to the straight up-and-down lines of a steam locomotive, or a streamlined Cord motorcar to the hulking boxlike frame of a tin lizzie. And the same observation might be made of the bread box or the coffee grinder or the tea kettle—each noticeably more horizontal and curved than its counterparts of 1929 or 1932.

Washing machine (*left*) designed by Henry Dreyfuss for Associated Merchandising Corporation, 1934. Streamlined Cadillac-Fleetwood coupe (*opposite*), 1937.

"We are rounding the corner," the noted furniture designer Kem Weber wrote in 1936, punning consciously on both the basic shape of the decade and on its salutary effect upon an embattled economy. Everything from radios and mirrors to washing machines and ladies' hats was by that time sporting the new rounded look—a look which affected even Hollywood's ideal of feminine beauty. As hopelessly out of vogue as a dialless, vertical telephone was the angular face of a Katharine Hepburn, who, in 1938, was labeled "box-office poison," in part because she in no way resembled such stylish moon-faced lovelies as Rochelle Hudson and Arline Judge. And, if the rounded face was not the new ideal, how else explain the contemporary popularity of those chinless singing zeroes, Harriet Hilliard and Frances Langford? Or of that skating cipher, Sonja Henie? But we are racing ahead in time to the end of a decade before examining its start.

What rational explanation, we ask, can be found for this singular phenomenon, a change in the preference for shapes that informed an age? And what has it to do with the Great Depression?

America, in spite of the Depression, and perhaps because of it, had looked around and found itself shabby and wanting, its tastes and forms determined, largely, by influences from abroad, its production geared to meet the needs of a passing social order. Its tastemakers, the millionaires who were willing to go back 3,000 miles or 300 years for their choicest possessions, no longer existed in any great number, and those who did, those who still controlled American corporations and industry, were now understandably prejudiced against sending their capital to foreign shores. They looked

instead to economic recovery through the development of a new set of wants, through an American appetite for things both fresh and new. The result, nurtured in the depths of the Depression, was a new materialism, fostered by a new breed of creative designer to whom an America of industriousness, material progress, and opportunity was no mere myth. Out of their talents and creative efforts, and through the peculiarly American marriage of art and industry, came an impulse toward forms that were fresh and intelligent. Forms that grew out of current needs, instead of archaic needs. Forms that assimilated new materials and functioned to meet contemporary wants. This new materialism, turning its back on the luxuriousness of the 1920s,

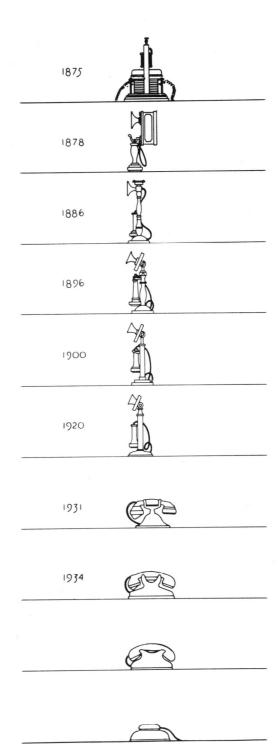

1875

1878

1886

1896

1900

1920

1931

1934

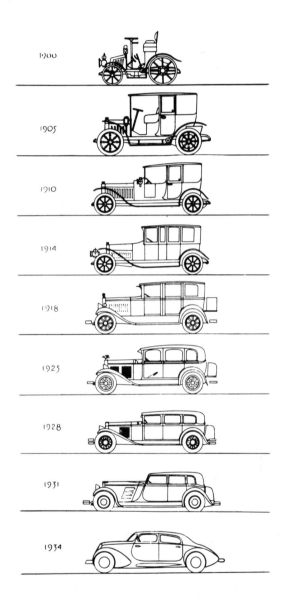

1900

1905

1910

1914

1918

1925

1928

1931

1934

and concentrating on simpler, more useful objects, reflected an authentic social mood, an attitude of interest in things created expressly for its peculiar age. And out of it—in automobile and railroad train, in home and in office, in department store and corner shop—developed the identifying features of a style as different from the Art Deco of the 1920s as it is similar to its offspring in the 1970s.

Because of these physical correspondences, because of the many similarities between the landscape of material objects then and now, the era of the Great Depression is ultimately far closer to us in experiential time than the year 1901 was in measured time to Thornton Wilder's audience. Even if Hollywood escapists did occasionally exploit as sexual metaphor the ta-ra-ra-boom-de-ay of the gilded '90s, it is hard to imagine during the Depression a widespread nostalgia for the year 1901. There was none, in fact. America in the 1930s, down on its luck, but believing nonetheless in the material benefits of mechanized progress, sought its way out of the Depression not through a nostalgic return to its preindustrial past, but through the creation of new objects, of needed and necessary things, well designed and inexpensively mass-produced. While some sang cynically of paper moons on cardboard seas, others dreamed, optimistically, of an American Era in which everyone, rich and poor alike, would share in the material riches of the nation—of a time in which all Americans would own a multitude of simple, useful, beautiful objects bought in stores created consciously as a golden mean between the five-and-dime and Tiffany's.

We are materialists, most of us. In recognizing how much closer we are to 1938 in our mundane likes and wants than 1938 was to 1901, we can begin to understand our present fascination with the years of the Great Depression. The parallels are all too obvious, even if superficial. Business is down. Unemployment is up. Social concerns are high. "Movements" are rife. Most of us want more, not less; sooner, not later. Everyman his own Henry Fonda. Everywoman her own Sylvia Sidney. In the face of corruption and ineptitude in high places, of public scandal and private disaster, the new Forgotten Man awaits a new leader, a new savior, an apocalyptic symbol fluttering blue and aery wings in a Busby Berkeley sky—an NRA eagle for the 1970s.

In these correspondences—both emotional and mundane—we are all, in a sense, children of the '30s, our eyes still earthbound despite the recent conquest of the moon. After all, to a generation raised on matinees at the Pix or the Luxor or the Bijou, didn't Buster Crabbe accomplish even greater interplanetary feats every Saturday afternoon?

Let us now move backward in time. And to Paris.

"J'suis Français, j'suis Chauvin." Chauvinism—irrevocably French by dint of its very derivation—is a highly justifiable national trait when it comes to assessing Art Deco. For the French, and the French only, have a right to claim Deco as their own.

To have entered the fashionable salons of Paris in the decade before 1925, to have walked within the houses in the Faubourg St. Honoré or within the shops in the Boulevard des Capucines, was to marvel at the opulence of a Tamerlane, his riches plucked and plundered from the corners of the globe, or to comprehend in all their lush and lavish sensuousness the promises of Herod to his Salome. Here—amid Egyptian, Chinese, African, and Islamic *objets d'art*, scattered like rose petals at the feet of the epicene Heliogabalus—were furnishings wrought luxuriously in amboyna and in ivory, in Macassar ebony and silk brocade, in marbrite and Caucasian walnut, in repoussé leather or in silvered bronze. In their fine and detailed craftsmanship, each uniquely wrought for a single wealthy patron, the elegant pale sycamore and chrome furniture of Pierre Legrain, the inlaid ivory sofas of Marcel Coard, the moulded opalescent glass of René Lalique, the lacquered wood and ivory furniture of André Groult, or the sensuous sculptures of Gustav Miklos suggest nothing less than the royal court of *Le Roi Soleil*—Versailles resurgent, as it were, in 20th-century France.

Art Deco, then, is unmistakably French. And yet the term itself is English, a fact so obvious that it should give us pause.

We know, of course, that Art Deco derives its name from the great 1925 Paris exhibition, *L'Exposition Internationale des Arts Décoratifs et Industriels Modernes,* in which the style, in full flower, reached its culmination. We know, too, that the exhibition popularized this most conservative of styles and that the public embrace, antithetic to its exclusive nature, ultimately killed it. We know, finally, that today the term has somehow come to be applied to the complete range of artistic production of the 1920s and 1930s and that it is now applied equally, but indiscriminately, to the priceless furniture of

Clément Rousseau and to Bronx apartment houses, to junk jewelry and the covers of *Vogue*, to the Chrysler Building and the films of Rogers and Astaire.

What we forget, however, is that the French, precise as always, referred originally to the style as *l'art décoratif moderne*, carefully distinguishing the real thing from *le modernisme*: the style it became once it lost its sybaritic exclusivity and once it was reduced to a handful of surface motifs reproduced inexpensively for the masses. Curiously—but not so curiously once one thinks about it—both the English and the Americans have from the first referred to the style as "the modernistic." Until recently, that is. For the past fifteen years or so, we've been calling it Art Deco, a term that never existed in its own peculiar day.

Deco, like any rare plant, transplanted badly. It was brought back by Americans such as Donald Deskey and Joseph Urban, who discovered it in Paris, and by Europeans such as Frederick Kiesler and Josef Hoffmann and Paul Frankl, who foresaw America as a rich and logical ground for cultivation. Their works, commissioned in the late '20s by the Rockefellers and others similarly rich, remained true Deco—private, exclusive, luxurious. And, like anything else exclusive, there was precious little of it.

But others returned from Paris, too, ready to give the great American public its share of European smartness. Department store buyers, merchandisers, and fashion designers came back filled with enthusiasm, exotic color, and a few easily applied surface motifs. And what they created was called "the modernistic." Characterized, generally, by zigzags and asymmetrical patterning, it reduced the wealth and endless variety of Art Deco to a handful of decorative motifs: a squiggle here, a stylized sunburst there. True Deco had been soft, preferring lavish curves and curlicues in hand-wrought ballustrades and flower-patterned metal grillwork. But the modernistic was hard and largely angular, its zigzags and fluted columns far easier to stamp on machine-pressed objects from picture frames to refrigerator doors. Deco, characteristically understated, was dependent on a cumulative vision of luxury, each element in a room seen in relation to the whole effect. Deceptively subtle, it could be likened to a time bomb with a built-in detonator that required, merely, the sensory heat of sight and touch to activate it. The modernistic, however, all glittering surface and hollow substance, was more simply a bomb.

By 1930, the modernistic filled the lobbies of New York hotels and skyscrapers. It got into glassware and lipstick holders, compacts and cigarette cases. It altered advertising and the packaging of soap powders. It caused old-fashioned marble cake to change its name, for a day or two, to Cubist cake. It riddled the drug business—atomizers, perfume bottles, and other trifles were particularly hard hit. Even venerable commercial institutions tried it: Bon Ami Cleanser, abandoning in early 1929 its soft and fluffy baby chick ("It never scratches"), a trademark for almost half a century, replaced it with a black and yellow ziggurat, the ultimate in fashionable chic. Six months later the baby chick was back. And with it came the Great Depression.

Hard times bring with them the need, and the impulse, for stocktaking. America looked at itself and found itself fat. It felt the need for simplification. Gradually, therefore, the tide of the modernistic—the first wave of pseudo-modernism in America—began to ebb on every shore. On every shore, that is, but one. Hollywood had its own peculiar reason for holding on.

Early in its history, Hollywood had developed a visual vocabulary all its own, a pattern of symbols and conventions that spoke meaningfully, directly, and clearly to its audience, many of whom, because they could not read the subtitles of the silent cinema, would not have been able to follow the simple story line without these recognizable signposts. Long after the advent of sound had rendered them useless, Hollywood retained many of these conventions. And one of these visual symbols had to do with the modernistic vogue. It identified a particular moral evil. Until well into the '30s, every demimonde and every kept woman on the silver screen was always accommodated with a modernistic interior.

The modernistic Southtown Theater, Chicago, Illinois, 1931.

The equation was simple—"modern" equals sex —a formula all the more important in American films after William Randolph Hearst and all the other Forces of Good, attempting to put Mae West out of business, brought an end in Hollywood to sexual "explicitness," '30s-style. The very symbol of female license, therefore, whether in gangster's moll, banker's mistress, or high-priced whore, became the "smart" modernistic boudoir. Yards of white satin, a bed without posts, a chair without feet, and a mirror without frame—for the woman

1890
1900
1905
1910
1915
1920
1925
1930
1935

1650

1700

1730

1780

1810

1830

1880

1900

1920

1934

without morals. And, as an added mark of wantonness, the demimondes, when not in step-ins, seemed always to wear modernistic diamond clips on the straps of diaphanous nightgowns. It must have been painful to turn over in bed.

All the virtuous girls, of course—loyal wives, jilted sweethearts, innocent shopgirls, and all the other virgins—came out of sensible colonial bungalows, where they wrung their worried hands in chintz-covered sitting rooms or peered anxiously through lace-curtained windows, awaiting the return of fallen or transfigured heroes. And they never slept in beds. They only occasionally died in them.

Helped along by Hollywood, although gradually becoming moribund, the modernistic craze lasted into the early '30s. And well it should, since a 1932 automobile would have been designed in 1929, a 1932 skyscraper in 1928. But very early on, with the Depression deepening and the future looking bleak, with America tightening its belt and starting to think thin, the modernistic became a term of derision. After all, when William Van Alen, architect of the Chrysler Building, was called the "Ziegfeld of his profession," it wasn't meant to be a compliment.

The style which in its day was called Modern, but which I have chosen to call Depression Modern, developed out of several sources: economic, social, and artistic. But, essentially, it was a direct response to the vogue for the modernistic. It was, in fact, its very antithesis. The modernistic was a collection of motifs applied superficially to objects for the sole effect of novelty. In its quest for sophistication, for mere smartness, it masqueraded as something "modern." It was, however, merely eclectic, a watered-down borrowing of elements from the past which its predecessor, Art Deco, had earlier ransacked for its own magnificent needs. Depression Modern, on the other hand, was an art stripped bare of all ornamentation, an art in which the American home and office and factory—and everything in them—were built for just one purpose: to work, and to look as though they worked.

Ideally, the Depression Modern style was spare. Although the earliest examples did exhibit a certain amount of decorative detail, the style became purer and purer, until, finally, a Depression Modern house, or airplane, or chair, or chemical plant could be said to be without a single detail that could be called extraneous, without any embellishment, without a line that did not seem inevitable. There was nothing in Depression Modern to distract the eye or the mind. It was clean and uncluttered, direct and innocent.

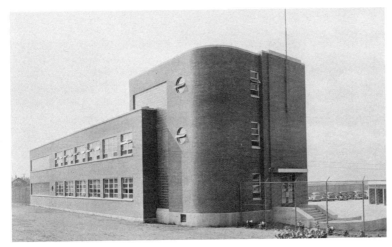

Administration building of Federated Metals Company, Hammond, Indiana, designed and built by The Austin Company, 1937.

The objectives of Depression Modern were efficiency, economy, and right appearance. Frequently these objectives were met; frequently they were not. Because the style was so directly related to the world of commerce, its chief designers and innovators were often required to compromise their ideals —sometimes against their will, more frequently with their consent. Many of these men and women became millionaires. Others did not. All of them shaped not only the world of the '30s, but our present day as well. In creating Depression Modern, a style which survived unchallenged until the late 1940s, they contributed, ultimately, to many contemporary wonders of technology. But, at their worst, they also planted some of the seeds that blossomed into the present *age de merde*. Consequently, both sides of Depression Modern—its achievements and its failures—are reflected in the photographs in this book.

Few generations have better understood themselves and their times than did the designers of the '30s. They knew what they were creating, they knew why they were creating it, and they even had a premonition of what their place in history would be because they had created it. They knew that they hated the modernistic. They knew that they were on to something different. And they knew that it was modern. Given the clarity and consistency of their vision and the number of primary sources in which their thoughts appeared, one wonders why popular history has included and continues to include them under the collective umbrella of the term Art Deco. Especially when they thought completely otherwise.

In support of this thought, one could quote from the published writings, or speeches, or notebooks of Raymond Loewy, Donald Deskey, Russel Wright, Walter Dorwin Teague, Vahan Hagopian, Dorothy Liebes, Marianne Willisch, Gilbert Rohde, or other designers of the Depression. But we can discover a great deal about the '30s just as well by taking a look at what was being taught in American schools of the period.

Astonishingly, a most wonderful description of the Depression Modern style has been preserved in the pages of a mere schoolgirl's notebook. It is correct in almost every point, even though it was taken down in childish Palmer penmanship by a teenage student in 1937. This is how the world of modern design looked to a homemaking class in a St. Paul, Minnesota, high school almost forty years ago:

> Different times and different countries have their own art. Modern is only a relative term. Things may be old-fashioned today and in the future be modern.
>
> What is modern and what is not modern is mainly governed by our ideals of beauty at that particular time.
>
> Art of today must be created today. It must express the life about us. Ours is a complex age. It is much more complex than any previous age. Invention, machinery, industry, science and commerce are characteristic of to-day. Individuals must have a way of relaxing from this complexity. Thus, we seek to surround ourselves with those things which have the effect of simplicity and which allow us to relax and forget our restlessness.
>
> The modern trend in design is an expression of a desire for honesty of materials, an escape from some of the imitative and over-decorated periods of the past.
>
> What is more natural and sensible, than to make the home simple, restful and easy to care for, to counteract the many demands of our social and business activities?
>
> *Design*—style is the expression of the times. Modernism is the style of reason, of square, of circle and horizontal line. Good forms and decoration together with good construction will always appeal.
>
> The smart modern today is as lightly and delicately scaled as are the Sheraton, Hepplewhite, and Adam designs in Georgian furniture, while still adhering to its original principle, that of functionalism.
>
> *Materials*—these new ideas demand new materials. One of the most conspicuous of these is glass which is used of itself, for itself, but not always by itself.
>
> It may be used as transparent glass, mirrors, and Vitrolite, which is black glass. Other new materials are Celanese and rayon, Monel metal—copper and nickel alloy—Bakelite—paper and rosin—lacquer fabrics, cork plates, linoleums, rubber flooring, aluminum, wall paper—Japanese veneer—French straw paper.
>
> Modernism is recognized by:
>> Simplicity
>> Unbroken lines
>> Use of pure colors
>> Contrasts in light and shadow
>> Honesty in materials: steel is steel, copper is copper and paint is recognized as paint and not made to resemble marble.

"Ours is a complex age." There is something poignant about these words, offered as they are as an explanation for the simplicity characteristic of the style of the 1930s. One wonders whether our St. Paul schoolgirl actually believed them or whether she was simply taking down, verbatim, her teacher's words. So removed in time from energy shortages, space exploration, and the threat of nuclear devastation, her thought suggests that simplicity in design was an escape, a refuge from the material world of the Depression, rather than a celebration of it, as was more likely the case.

On the contrary, most contemporary designers of the 1930s believed that in their time, nearly two hundred years after the start of the Industrial Revolution, America had for the first time shown a substantial accomplishment in relating machine-inspired design to a machine-inspired way of life. They believed that an earlier world, having come to an end in October 1929, placed them at the threshold of a new American era, one in which they, finally, were able to come to grips with the world of the machine. They believed that in creating new shapes and forms, simple and unornamented, they would succeed in adjusting humanely to a machine-driven world as their predecessors, in aping the eclectic styles and fashions of earlier periods, had failed.

The result of this belief, I think, was a succession of unusually shaped, but aesthetically pleasing, structures and objects that appeared during the Great Depression from coast to coast, in large city and small town, from Maine to California. Considering how the pioneering efforts of Sullivan and Wright had been largely ignored in their own country, the wide acceptance of the Depression Modern style marked probably the first—and, I lament, the last—time in America in which the purely functional was made to appear beautiful. It was surely the last successful attempt to realize the decorative inherent in the functional. And this was especially true of American industry, contemporary design having had its purest expression in the machine itself and then, logically, in its architectural counterpart, the factory.

The Church and Dwight factory, pictured in these pages, is a case in point. The owners of this company, makers of Arm & Hammer Baking Soda,

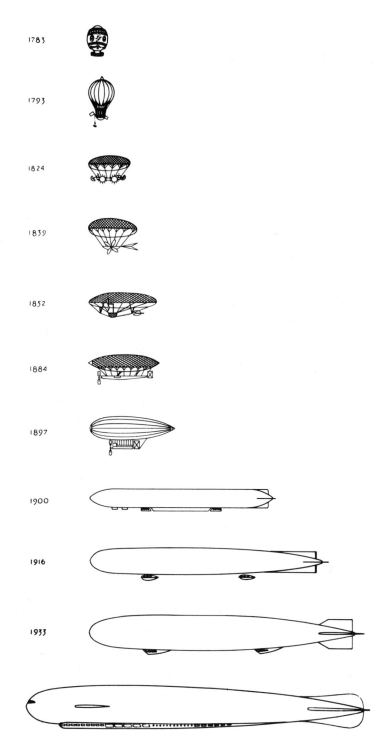

1783

1793

1824

1839

1852

1884

1897

1900

1916

1933

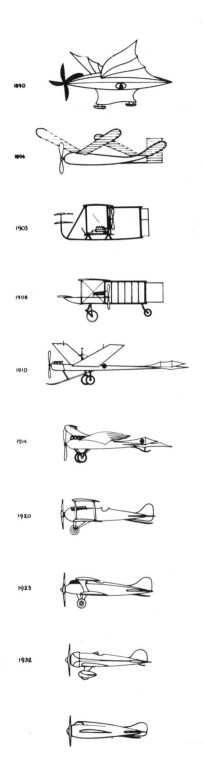

wanted a structure reflecting the purity of their product, and The Austin Company, consequently, designed a white brick, air-conditioned building in which the only ornament was its pattern of fenestration, a pattern dictated largely by function. The basic curve of the factory, that which gives it its singular shape, is purely functional: it is built around a seven-story industrial tank, necessary for the production of the company's product. To our eyes, the building appears as stark, as simple, and as primitively beautiful as it did in 1938. It could have been built only in a day that boasted of the essentially simple lines of its complex macadam

Church and Dwight factory, 1938.

parkways and cloverleafs, its bridges, and the massive, concrete dams of TVA.

"We achieve a high degree of simplicity because we are a primitive people," the designer Walter Dorwin Teague wrote in 1939. "We have reverted again to a primitive state of human development. We are primitives in this new machine age. We have no developed history behind us to use in our artistic creations. We have no theories, no vocabulary of ornament, behind us to use in our work. That is why so much of our modern work today has a certain stark and simple quality that relates it very closely to the primitive work of Greece and the primitive work of Egypt and the primitive work of most people who were discovering their techniques and their tools."

"We should be very careful to deny ourselves the luxury of decoration in the things that we do," Teague cautioned, "because we have no decoration today that is significant to us, that has a meaning. The Greeks, in their great day, in the design of the Parthenon, had at their command a vocabulary of ornament that they had inherited through years of work, that had become significant to them and was very useful in the creation of their internal rhythm. *But we have no ornament.*"

He was correct, of course. But the absence of an ornament for the modern day did not mean that lesser minds could not find one. And find one they did. Washing machines and apartment house façades, typewriters and gas pumps, space heaters and vacuum cleaners yielded their new unbroken surfaces to the strange cult of the "three little lines," three parallel lines intended to suggest "modernity" to the consumer, three parallel lines marring surfaces everywhere in America. Few objects of the '30s escaped the plague of this unholy trinity, suggesting one reason why the Depression Modern

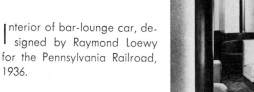

Interior of bar-lounge car, designed by Raymond Loewy for the Pennsylvania Railroad, 1936.

style is so frequently, and incorrectly, mistaken for the modernistic dilution of Art Deco. But these lines were far more than the modernistic zigzag gone straight. They were intended as a catch-all ornament for a day which rightly had no ornament.

Teague and his colleagues Norman Bel Geddes, Raymond Loewy, George Sakier, Russel Wright, Lurelle Guild, Eleanor LeMaire, and many others called themselves industrial designers, the very term "decorator" having become associated, pejoratively, with the effete luxuriousness of the antediluvian past. Most of them believed in "the rhythm of design," in the idea that the design of a period reflected, unconsciously, the spirit of an age. And in this belief they were undoubtedly correct. For it is a characteristic of any period that all of its creations have a certain family resemblance, an underlying unity of form which does not spring uniquely from the imagination of the artist, but rather reflects the surrounding world and especially the prevailing modes of production. The world of the 1930s was especially fond of a particular line, a curved line, recurring again and again, a line with a sharp parabolic curve at the end, which it called the "streamline." And it was the streamline which contemporary designers considered the characteristic "rhythm" of the age.

Streamlining, of course, had begun with the modern world's love of high speed. It was an attempt to increase the speed of moving mechanical objects by removing as many wind-deflecting obstacles as possible, designers having studied and observed the sleek, ovoid body of the porpoise and the unbroken surface of the teardrop. The first airplanes, trains, and automobiles had been vertical box-like affairs. By 1933, however, the modern streamlined ideal was the ovoid, gliding form and the smooth, continuous, unbroken surface of gleaming steel bodies. The speed of these new, sleek, streamlined vehicles caught the imagination of the public from the first display of the Burlington Zephyr at the Chicago World's Fair. And the subsequent appearance, throughout the decade, of other streamlined trains and ships and planes and motorcars made for lively page-one tabloid copy and for exciting footage in Paramount and Movie-tone newsreels. Americans, then even more than now, lived vicariously.

Streamlining, ultimately, became the vogue—and a way of marketing items which were never designed with speed in mind. Furniture and clothing, clocks and typewriters, electric irons and toasters, even false teeth and coffins, were hawked to Depression consumers as "streamlined," even though, with the possible exception of coffins, none was designed to transport its owner anywhere, at any speed. Although we may easily ridicule the commercial perversion of the streamline theory as typical of an age that was considerably less than golden, the streamline vogue was nevertheless an inherent reflection of the spirit of the decade. "Now, one reason why we are streamlining so many things today," Teague wrote in 1939, "things which will never move and have no excuse for being streamlined in the sense that they need to be adapted to the flow of air currents, is simply because of the dynamic quality of the line which occurs in streamline forms, and it is characteristic of our age. We are a primitive age, a dynamic people, and we respond only to the expressions of tensions, of vigor, of energy. And this line occurs constantly throughout our bodies—a muscular male body or a beautifully formed female body."

Teague's words, so simple and direct, suggest the WPA murals then being painted in post offices, courthouses, and other public buildings throughout America: graphic panoplies, symbolic mosaics of ocean liners and airplanes, of bridges and highways, of iron foundries and assembly lines, and, everywhere, the muscular figures of bare-chested men and Amazonian women, workers all for material prosperity and the national good.

No. Depression America adopted simple forms not as an escape from its complex age, but, rather, as a celebration of it.

"New ideas," our St. Paul schoolgirl had written, "demand new materials." And if Art Deco had plundered the riches of the world in its pursuit of luxury, if it had doted on amboyna and ivory and shagreen, on rare fabrics and even rarer woods, then Depression Modern, in its pursuit of the elegantly simple, of the direct and the useful, created its own materials. And most of them were machine-made. For the 1930s was, above all, a decade of alloys and of steel, of plastics and of glass. No wonder documentary films of the time favored montages to symbolize the mechanical progress of America: molten metals and blazing furnaces, whirring presses and hair-netted assembly-line women, gushing oil wells, and Brobdingnagian reapers decimating amber fields of grain—God, as it were, crowning the nation's good with Prosperity and ball bearings.

If the Depression had produced a Walt Whitman to catalogue its sights and sounds, its movement and its spirit, the poet would have heard a new America singing. And singing a new song—its vocabulary a scramble of Latin and Greek suffixes and chemical terms, its words as synthetic as the substances they describe, a litany to the scientific wonders of the age. Celluloid, Pyralin, Fiberloid, and Nixonoid for combs and buckles, buttons and dresser sets. Tenite, Plastacele, and Lumarith for lamp shades, watch crystals, bathroom accessories, fountain pens, and eyeglass frames. Ameroid for cigarette holders, chessmen, buttons, ashtrays, and piano keys. Vinylite for floor tile, toothbrushes, synthetic glass, and steering wheels. Coltrock and Bakelite, Durez and Durite, Insurok and Indur, Makalot and Resinox, Textolite and Arcolite for clocks and automobile parts, telephone instruments and typewriter parts, door knobs, kettle handles, radio cases, and electrical parts. Catalin, Marblette, Ivaleur, and Fiberloid for costume jewelry, cutlery handles, buttons, buckles, knobs, and rods of synthetic glass. Micarta, Formica, Textolite, Lamicoid, Panelyte, Insurok, Synthane, Dilecto, Phenolite, and Spauldite for store fronts, table tops, radiator covers, paneled walls, doors, sink tops, and automobile parts.

And in the world of glass there were Aklo and Tuf-flex, Vitrolux and Thermolux, Thermopane and Vitrolite, Glastone and Extrudalite. Heat-absorbing glass and sculptured glass. Tempered and laminated glass. Fiber glass and ultra-violet glass. Invisible glass and one-way glass. Colored mirror glass in peach and blue, in gunmetal and gold. And, above all, there was glass block. Everywhere.

Used abroad for many years, particularly in Holland, glass block (sometimes called brick) won a rather belated acceptance in the United States by 1935, becoming, finally, the most firmly established material of modern building, in part because

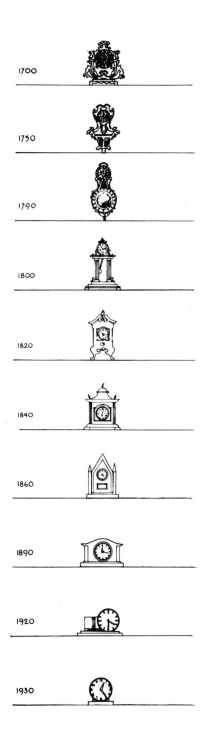

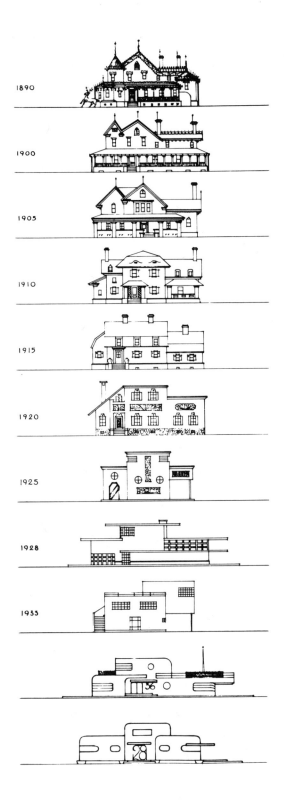

1890

1900

1905

1910

1915

1920

1925

1928

1933

it lent itself less readily to stylistic adaptations than any building material that had yet appeared. Its very existence demanded a "modern" setting. Used as wall or window, as inner partition or simple decoration, for bar or soda fountain, and even (for the fanciful) in furniture, glass block gave translucence without visibility, light with little heat transmission (making it perfect for America's first air-conditioned buildings), effective sound insulation, and low maintenance costs since it required no finish.

In the late 1930s, America's leading manufacturer of glass block publicized its product in trade magazines by building a glass Depression Modern playhouse, a veritable fantasy of Insulux, for Shirley Temple. In magazine advertisements that must have startled conservative architects, the dimpled moppet was shown, trowel in pudgy hand, building a towering glass-block structure, her smile of easy childish confidence antedating the Castro Convertible girl by at least a decade. Glass block, enormously popular in its day, vanished from the scene at about the same time that Shirley Temple did. But both, like them or not, were hallmarks of their age.

In metals and plastics, in cork and glass—new materials for new ideas. And even old materials were re-explored to serve the new: wood and nickel, aluminum and leather providing texture, grain, vibration, glint, and glow—all necessary for an art that preferred no ornamentation if it were to be considered new. Let us not for a minute underestimate the American public's fascination with things new and inventive. Let us not forget Barnum's fable of the Egress. Cellophane, a sensation when exhibited at Chicago's Century of Progress Exposition in 1933, was no less exciting six years later when used in a publicity stunt that could have taken place in no other decade. To celebrate the opening of the first community of

Levitt houses on Long Island, and, of course, to promote sales, the entire chorus line of Broadway's *Babes in Arms* appeared in force, each with a pair of enormous scissors, to inaugurate a shiny, new model home. It had been wrapped, from top to bottom, in cellophane. An enormous, glittering gift-wrapped package, topped with a huge plastic bow. And this while Christo was still in rompers. In 1939 they called it a publicity stunt. Today we call it art.

Mass education in America, especially on the college level, has produced a cultural game for our times, a game, for lack of a better name, called "Associations." And this has come about because postgraduate cultural life is little more than a random, but never-ending, short-answer quiz, a continuation of art and literature and music served up raw in textbooks and in lecture halls, the mass regurgitated and ill-digested. The mark of an educated man today is measured by his ability to come up with the right set of "associations" or responses to a given list of artists' names, identifying in turn the artist's field and, for extra points, the titles of his works. According to the rules of the game, if one can name an author and match him with the titles of his books, one is, ipso facto, educated—whether one has read the author's work or not.

Most of us have more than once overheard the game in progress, or even innocently participated in it, over drinks at the country club, or at a cocktail party, or while queuing up to see the latest trendy Mel Brooks film. We've heard it over restaurant tables, or at the office coffee machine, or amid the babble and chatter of TV talk shows. "Picasso," one bored man says to another. "Modern artist—*Guernica*," the other responds, equally bored. Ten points and another sip of scotch. "Debussy." "French composer—*La Mer*." Fifteen points and back to the golf game. "Ingmar Bergman." "Swedish director. Very interesting." Five points: incomplete, but cogent; accurate and masterfully concise. And so it goes, the names changing every season to remain in touch with the ins and outs of popular culture. "Art Deco." "The 1930s."

Ask any hundred educated Americans the names of two important designers of modern furniture (or even one) and chances are that thirty will be able to do so. And, of those thirty, twenty-nine will almost certainly mention Le Corbusier, Marcel Breuer, or Mies van der Rohe, Europeans all. The chance is probably zero that anyone will bring up the names of the American designers Donald Deskey, Gilbert Rohde, Kem Weber, or Russel Wright. And this is only natural in a culture which sees itself, still, as stepchild to its Continental masters.

The formidable accomplishments of Mies, Breuer, and Corbu notwithstanding, this native inferiority complex is indeed a pity. For at the very time in which the superb creations of the three Europeans were being meticulously handcrafted for a small, but discriminating clientele, Deskey's metal-tubing chairs were already being turned out by the thousands at a Grand Rapids factory, and the other three

Americans were in the process of designing mass-produced furniture of sound proportion, simple finish, and structural integrity—furniture that would radically change the appearance of the American home, and in numbers that would have astonished the European designers. In the conception of their furniture, neither Deskey, nor Weber, nor Rohde, nor Wright had been directly influenced by European models, and all four were attempting nothing less than the creation of a modern American style.

Of the four, the most versatile was Donald Deskey, his life a continuous round of inventive genius, interrupted only by retirement at the age of 80. Those who glibly play "Associations," if they know his name at all, will respond invariably with the fact that Deskey had designed the interiors of Radio City Music Hall. An achievement, to be sure. But only one, and hardly the most important, in a career spanning more than five decades.

Some day a book will be written about Deskey, his life and his accomplishments, and it will have as its title, one hopes, *Contemporary American,* an apt description of the man himself and also the punch line of a frequently told, but true, story about him—a story which tells us worlds about the goals of modern American design in its early days. Already famous at the age of thirty, Deskey, in the late 1920s, had created for a conservative manufacturer a modern room in which revolutionary use had been made of cork, asbestos, glass, and metal, the total effect of which was extremely simple. A visitor, shown Deskey's room, his eyes open wide with astonishment, commented with surprise on the manufacturer's sudden interest in "the new modern style." "That's not modern style," the manufacturer replied, "that's good contemporary American."

Good contemporary American. This was the ideal not only of Donald Deskey, but of the entire movement of Depression Modern, an ideal seeking expression in architecture and in machinery, in transportation and in furnishings—an ideal implying honesty, and simplicity, and functional expressiveness. And it had its most demonstrable impact, perhaps, in home furnishings—in accessories and, especially, in the design of modern American furniture.

In periods of transition, such as that of the Great Depression, it takes considerable time for the changes wrought in social and economic life to find a general expression in the arts. It is, in fact, a basic law that the creative expression of an era must conform to the general development of that period. The creative artist, after all, senses new directions long before the public becomes aware of them, and he realizes that the new and contemporary expression in art only reflects the change in modes of living in which each individual himself takes active part. For this reason, at the threshold of a new era, Americans, in the first years of the Great Depression, found themselves with an already well-developed modern outlook toward life, one born of economic necessity, but with a correspondingly conservative inclination toward modern art.

As a consequence, then, Depression Modern did not take hold over night. It was through small things, through accessories—through glassware, pottery, metalware, table linens, and woodenware—that modern design found its first wide-scale success in America. The repeal of Prohibition in 1933, perhaps more than any other single event, led multitudes of Americans to the back door of contemporary design. It introduced Americans—and particularly the American woman—to the new social institution of the cocktail hour, an event for which designers created the cocktail shaker, the ice bucket, the snack tray, and an assortment of inventions deemed necessary for enjoying the new pastime. Drinking, for America, became superbly modern, and most of its new forms reflected good contemporary design. Once invaded, the American home was vulnerable. And as it became increasingly populated with ultra-modern ice tongs and cheese boards, pitchers and ashtrays, all created of shimmering new materials, all as modern as Amelia Earhart, the next logical place in which Depression Modern could succeed was in the world of American furniture itself.

The average American couple, beginning married life in the early '30s, bought a suite of machine-made bedroom furniture, decorated most frequently in mock Tudor or Stuart or Italian Renaissance style. Characterized by indifferent design, poor construction, and even poorer materials, such suites were known in the trade, with more than just a little contempt, as "borax"—a wonderful American term that has all but vanished from the language. Because hawkers of the then-famous cleanser, Twenty Mule Team Borax, had offered as free premiums cheap and garish kitsch, the word "borax" came to be associated with the "extra" values offered by commercial furniture manufacturers: "extra" carving, "extra" large-size frames, "extra" glossy finish.

For more than three generations in America, from furniture showroom to the pages of Montgomery Ward, one bought a "suite" of furniture, more frequently pronounced "suit." For more than three generations, a bedroom suite consisted of a dresser, a vanity, a chest, and a bed. A dining room suite consisted of a buffet, a china closet, a server, a table, and six chairs. Regardless of the change in the life or tastes of the people, borax or refined, the form remained essentially the same, year in and year out. Manufacturers put Chippendale ornament on a dresser and called it Chippendale, despite the fact that Chippendale had never designed anything even vaguely resembling a

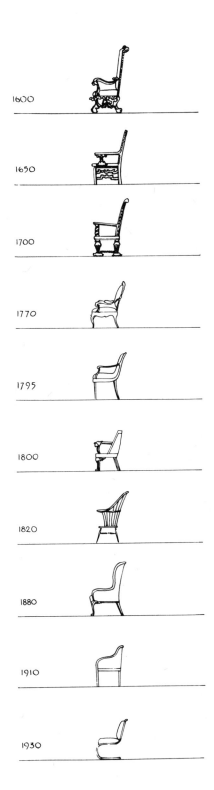

1600

1650

1700

1770

1795

1800

1820

1880

1910

1930

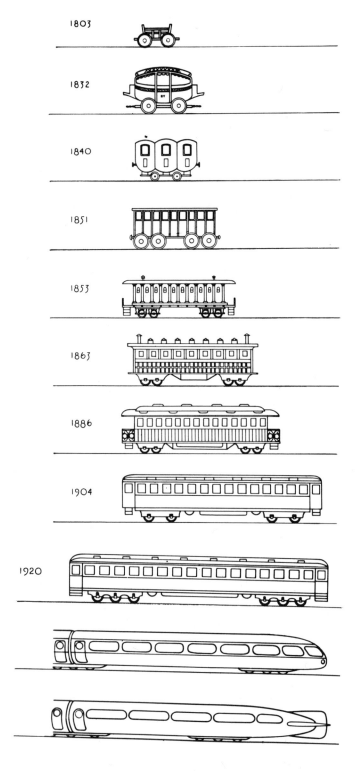

dresser. On the same basic form they put Span- ish, or Adam, or Queen Anne decoration, and changed the name of the style accordingly. By changing the faces on the same chassis, they had borax, or highly ornate, or any period style the public wanted. But then came the Great Depres- sion, and, with it, its all-embracing revolution in design.

With every major change in economics or poli- tical life has come a new period in furniture. And the Depression brought no exception to the rule. America was in a new economic and political era, and styles were changing all about it. By 1933, the same pattern we have already witnessed was forcefully in progress: designs, once created exclu- sively for the wealthy in the late '20s, were being mass-produced inexpensively for the common man of the '30s. What visitors to the Century of Prog- ress Exposition witnessed in the year in which FDR replaced Hoover was a dynamic demonstra- tion of a new artistic principle: a New Deal, as it were, for the world of American design—a belief, almost religious in its fervor, that modern design could be a means of improving the quality of con- temporary life. What fairgoers saw was something as new in furniture as the Burlington Zephyr had been in transportation. Modern American furniture, although it never ceased completely to be sold in suites, was now being offered in individual pieces that could be grouped or fitted into the needs of the newer, smaller, servantless, more efficient American home. In the highly commercial world of mass-produced furniture, the interchangeable unit, the modular, the sectional—that which we so take for granted today—was finally born.

The appearance of sectional furniture offered flexibility to a depressed industry and economy to a consumer who could now only infrequently afford the purchase of an entire matching suite. Early in the decade, Gilbert Rohde created for the

Herman Miller Furniture Company a complete "plan for comfortable living," which featured small units that could be combined and rearranged into innumerable schemes of interior decoration, making a good deal of variety possible on a single investment, and including chests designed intelligently as ensembles so that the consumer could use one, two, or three to fit any wall space. At about the same time, in 1933, Russel Wright's many-sided furniture and three-piece sectional sofas for Heywood-Wakefield illustrated the identical principle of functional versatility.

If any one person in the '30s best represents Depression Modern as more than just a commercial development, but as a social force straining for a better home for a happier people, then it is Russel Wright. And no other designer of the period more clearly represents the contemporary quest for a modern native-American style. His address before the New York Fashion Group in 1938 reveals his vision in all the forcefulness of its youthful vigor. In it, he tells the wonderful story of how, in having visited the handsome Bauhaus exhibit at the Museum of Modern Art a few days before, he had bumped into a German acquaintance, who accused American designers of being artistically backward. They were backward, he declared, because their work consisted entirely of copies of designs that had been executed in Germany years ago. Wright, as he tells the story, quietly fumed, his blood reaching the boiling point:

> My thoughts raced backward over personal experiences. Years of learning that Europe was the source of all culture. And then of finally going to Europe, rejoicing and reveling in the treasures there. Years of learning to talk in parrot fashion about Old World charm and New World barbarism. And then at last my sudden discovery as I looked again at our skyscrapers—our buildings and streets, our fat farm buildings, our gleaming rivers of traffic that I had not seen for months. I realized that America does have a very definite character of its own—that in all that we make here is a distinct visual pattern decidedly different from anything Europe does. Although our work is usually crude and raw, we seem to have our own conception of scale and it is grander than the European conception; our use of form is bolder and more vital; our use of color is distinctly our own.
>
> Why, then, must our museums and our art schools and our press and our critics still look to Europe; why must Europe always be advanced to us as the criterion? Why must our designers and our artists suffer most of their lives under the handicap of America's inferiority complex? Why don't they look around them? . . .
>
> Why can't someone, a Museum of Modern Art or a New York World's Fair, put on an exhibit in which they would dramatize all design that is American? First, let them parade those unconscious developments free from any aesthetic inferiority complexes. Our bridges. Our roads. Our factory machinery. Our skyscrapers. Let them throw a spotlight on our shining bathrooms and our efficient kitchens. Roll out our trick cocktail gadgets—our streamlined iceboxes—our streamlined pencil sharpeners. Let them show our electric light bulbs on white velvet like jewels. The work of Frank Lloyd Wright. Our gasoline stations. Our movie theatres. Our cafeterias. No matter how vulgar they are. Our handsome business machines. Our sport clothes. Our particular brand of shooting galleries and barber shops. Our gleaming fat automobiles. Then let them arrange our home furnishings in this parade. Let them put a magnifying glass (if they feel they need it) over these things to find the American character. But I am sure that they will not need it for the continuity of character will then become apparent. Let them do this without recourse to European standards in their selection. It has never been done. But I know that they will find that there is a distinct American character of design in all that is American and that our home furnishings *tie in to this character.* Not until then, will we know of what elements this American character consists.
>
> Rid yourselves of the American inferiority complex, forget European standards, look at the American scene, and *have more respect for it.*

Russel Wright, then only thirty-four years old, was speaking from long, personal experience, as the creator of "American Modern," a unique line of furniture—the most popular produced during the Depression, and the one that made his name a commonplace in tens of thousands of American homes.

"American Modern" furniture, created first in 1935 for the Conant-Ball Company and popularized by R. H. Macy, was an almost immediate commercial success. It grew out of Wright's long-stated belief that America had to reject European tradition in order to relate the functional modern style, so prevalent abroad, to its own needs. In forcing himself to examine these American needs, he determined that Americans, faced with a raging economic Depression, were working out new ways of living and in so doing were eliminating the useless and the invalid values of an outmoded culture. In trying to simplify their lives, Americans were trying to become more efficient. And of their new surroundings they were now demanding honest value, simplicity, sturdiness, and new innovations pertaining to comfort. These, he believed, were the basic requisites of American taste. Because of its mechanical facility, because of its dominant spirit of enterprise and its basic lack of Old World tradition, America was ripe for the development of a national style. And Wright's contribution to this style was his famous line of "American Modern" furniture—a line followed in succession by fabrics, bedspreads, lamps, table linen, china, glass, and giftware, all bearing the same name or its later variant, as war broke out in Europe, the "American Way."

"American Modern" bedroom, 1935.

Attempting to discover modern design of inherently American character, Wright turned to maple—the wood of the pioneer forefathers, which, because of its availability, strength, and hard surface, had been used since colonial times for furniture making. But it was not until 1935, and the advent of "American Modern," that maple came into its own for contemporary furniture. Wright's use of solid lumber uncovered by veneer helped not only to bring down production costs for modern furniture, but tended also to provide for greater freedom of design, facilitating, for instance, the rounded or cushion edge which became, ultimately, one of the identifying features of 1930s furniture. His return to full, hardy craftsmanlike forms gave his maple designs great adaptability to a large number of American homes, enabling "American Modern" to fit compactly into a small apartment or to be used more expansively in larger homes.

Wright was largely responsible, too, for the enormous popularity of light-colored woods in the '30s, for, with his "American Modern," he was the first to use a bleached maple finish for commercial furniture, calling it (at his wife's suggestion) "blonde," a term which became almost synonymous with American furniture of the late '30s and which paved the way for the invasion of "Swedish Modern" that ended the decade.

The "American Modern" line, in units that could be purchased separately and inexpensively, included living room, sunroom, dinette, and bedroom furniture. With its curves and flowing lines, this innovative furniture broke away completely from the geometric, packing-box type of modern so common at the beginning of the decade, nonetheless fulfilling the basic precepts of modern design, its careful proportions following the basic requirements of use and comfort. Russel Wright's "American Modern" furniture, perhaps more successfully than any other design of the decade, attempted to break out of the confining straightjacket of imitated European modernism, creating in its place a modern furniture with a strong affinity for the American home. If Wright believed that he had succeeded in creating a basic "American Modern" design, then thousands of Americans agreed with him.

Inevitably, their children and grandchildren thought otherwise. For "American Modern," and its many imitators, can be found now, battered and worn, in thriftshops and Salvation Army stores all over the nation.

7

Main Street. Any small city, U.S.A. The present.

The street lies bare, littered, crumbling. Its buildings, boarded and deserted, await the wrecker's ball, the looter's sack. In days or weeks, the sun will shine for the first time in half a century on three-story buildings a block away. In two years, or maybe three, a ribbon of highway, cars and trucks breathing fumes of black carbon, will bisect the city, its traffic passing from here to there, from there to here, as if the city no longer existed. These are the streamlined cars of yesterday. And this is its Main Street.

The Superette, where food stamps lately marked the closing of the city's aerosol-spray plant, was once The Gem, where posters, advertising *Rosemarie* and "Wednesday Bank Night," were affixed to green Micarta walls. Beneath the grit-encrusted glass block of the padlocked Erin Bar & Grill lie the cracked shards of Vitrolite, black and shattered. A group of squatters, patient until the end, play dominoes on ancient wooden milk crates before the storefront *Iglesia de Jesus,* once Gus's Bake Shop and, in 1933, the first "modern" store in town, its remodeled façade of stainless steel and glass superimposed upon the dull red brick of a late-Victorian building. And then the Carlton-Pickwick Restaurant, its elegant Thermolux and Formica interiors and its flesh-tinted rounded mirrors long ago replaced by the simulated stone, brick, and wood of a later day—all three textures falsely plastic and all grotesquely mixed, beneath fake colonial chandeliers, in the anarchistic style of the 1960s.

The Carlton-Pickwick. Gus's Bake Shop. The Gem. This might have been the very street on which my parents strolled the night they decided to marry and to face the Depression together more than forty years ago.

My mother and father, like America's Main Street, like the Broadway of Thornton Wilder's *Our Town*, are dead. America, always careless of its past, has been particularly cruel to the authentic heritage of the Depression, never, after all, having really loved it, never having wanted to be reminded of it. It has been abandoned to the modern carrion—to the romantics, to the distorters, to the collectors of kitsch.

The odd mirror-covered building on Times Square, its blue-tinted glass once reflecting the excitement of the Crossroads of the World, is like the windows of Ecclesiastes—blind, unseeing—its glass long ago shattered into thousands of pieces. Curtain time on the new Broadway is no longer at 8:30. And the theater where *Our Town* opened on February 4, 1938, Henry Miller's Theater, is now a hard-core pornographic movie house, late shows Friday and Saturday at midnight.

My parents lie dead, buried beneath a stone which my mother had designed at my father's death, never herself having lived to see its completion. Surrounding them, so unlike the graveyard scene in *Our Town*, with its black umbrellas and its dead conversing from wooden folding chairs, are the tombstones of my family—cold marble, bearing names existing only in memory and faces recorded in the fading pictures of my family album. An aunt, whom I had never known, murdered at fourteen in 1932. A second-cousin, the victim of meningitis, dead at eight in 1933. The bearded old man, for whom I'm named, asleep since 1937. My father's father, one of thousands struck down in 1918 by the influenza epidemic, and the first to be buried in the crowded cemetery from a motor-driven hearse, the single greatest distinction of his thirty-seven years, and the only fact that I have ever learned of his history in my thirty-seven years. And, standing like mute soldiers in row on silent row, the graves of others, whose eerie oval photographs, mounted under glass upon their 1920s stones, continually walk the corridors of my childhood dreams.

So strange to notice that these gravestones, like everything else in the coldly material world, bear the signs and symbols of the times in which they were made. How odd and grimly humorous, that death, like life, should observe the vogues and fashions of the day. The stone of 1932, probably already old-fashioned when it was chosen by a Depression family grieving for its youngest child so cruelly slain, is clearly modernistic, a vertical ziggurat in black and gray, its angular lines celebrating the suddenness of earthly loss. My grandfather's stone is nondescript, a borrowing of the classical and traditional, as eclectic as anything created in that final year of World War I, sentimental but cold, a monument to the ubiquity of death. My namesake's gravestone, curved and white, a simple and direct marker for a simple man, is plainly Depression Modern, its graceful lines suggesting the infiniteness of eternal rest.

But, as I look upon this 1937 stone, so sleek (dare I say streamlined?), I smile in recognition of its single ornament, three slender parallel lines. The cult of the unholy trinity. It has left its mark upon my namesake's grave and, hence, on me.

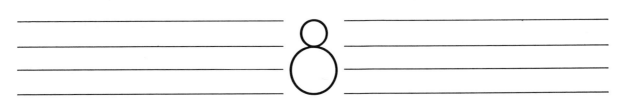

August 12, 1939. The pages of *The New Yorker*. The sophisticated column, "The Talk of the Town."

Looking at one of the newer buses, streamlined to cleave the trade winds that sweep Fifth Avenue, we wondered again what another generation will think of the bogus functionalism which seems to be the keynote of our own. We can remember our grandmother's house quite clearly. Outside, it was an atrocity of scrollwork and irrelevant turrets; inside, a dim museum in which animal and vegetable matter decayed quietly and respectably, under glass; altogether it was the typical house of its time. It was absurd, but it was saved from vulgarity by its innocence, and we still think of it with affection; and, because its furnishings were always rational though often hideous, we can easily imagine what it would have been like to live there. This nostalgia, we feel, is going to be a little harder for the grandchildren of many of our contemporaries. How to account, except by a sort of mass insanity, for a generation that designed everything, from automobiles to alarm clocks, to buffet a hypothetical tornado? How to picture one's ancestors, warm and alive, in all that steely symmetry? It is inevitable that the American home, in its current design, will presently come to be regarded as old-fashioned, but it is hard to believe that it will be remembered with love or pleasure. If your grandchildren think of you at all, surrounded by your bright, functional toys, it will be with terror or dislike, as a madman or stranger.

August 12, 1939. The very same page of *The New Yorker*. The very same sophisticated column ridicules with polite laughter an installment of Chester Gould's *Dick Tracy*, in which "the last picture shows the villains, a couple of fake European ambassadors, discovering a secret message concealed in the olive of a Martini cocktail." *O tempora! O mores!* How Watergate has stilled the laughter of such ridicule.

As H. L. Mencken once observed, "The prophesying business is like writing fugues; it is fatal to everyone save the man of absolute genius."

Let it suffice that no one on the distinguished *New Yorker* staff ever wrote a fugue.

Terror and dislike? Madmen and strangers? Hardly. Let the pages that follow speak of love and pleasure.

THE THIRTIES STYLE IN AMERICA

AN ALBUM

Design of the 1930s, from painting and sculpture to architecture and home furnishings, had its most important basis in the widely varied elements of American industry. The structures most closely related to industry, therefore, represent the peak of Depression architecture, factories in particular illustrating the contemporary trend toward simplicity and directness.

Among the most distinguished and extraordinary of American modern industrial buildings were those designed and constructed by The Austin Company of Cleveland, Ohio, whose advertisements in *Fortune* magazine throughout the Great Depression stood out above all others in their stunning—even startling—modernity. The Austin Company's structures of the 1930s remain to this day magnificent archetypes of the functional Depression Modern style. To see one is to experience in a moment the very "feel" of the period. The architectural models pictured here were constructed between 1936 and 1939.

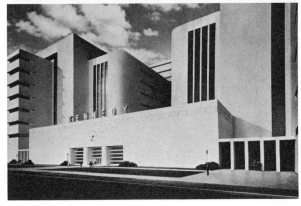

Built in 1937, the Hecht Company warehouse, Washington, D.C. (*above*), and the Campana Sales Company factory, Batavia, Illinois (*center*), won mention in the prestigious Pittsburgh Glass Institute competition of that year. In the warehouse, glass block functions as wall and window, while, in the factory, it is effectively combined with terra-cotta facing. The warehouse was designed by Abbot, Merkt & Co.; the factory, by Childs & Smith and Frank D. Chase, associated architects.

Research laboratory of American Rolling Mill Co. (above), Middletown, Ohio, design and construction by The Austin Company, 1937.

Johnson & Johnson's Industrial Tape Building (*top*), New Brunswick, New Jersey, R. G. and W. M. Cory, architects, 1940. *Center:* Wyatt Clinic and Research Laboratories Building, Tucson, Arizona, Leland W. King, Jr., architect, 1935. *Right:* Forest Products Laboratory, Madison, Wisconsin, Holabird & Root, architects, 1933.

While most industries were foundering during the Great Depression, radio was burgeoning. In 1936, NBC constructed the "latest" in studios for its Hollywood station. It was outmoded before it was occupied. Its replacement, in 1938, was The Austin Company's "Radio City of the West" (*left*). Not to be outrivaled, CBS engaged the architect William Lescaze to design its Hollywood studios (*above, top*), completed in 1938, one year after its KNX transmitter (*above*) opened in the same city.

Corning-Steuben Building (*left*), New York City, 1937. In the structure and decoration of this building, designed by William & Geoffrey Platt and John M. Gates, the company's own products were utilized to the fullest extent: of the limestone walls which enclose the offices, 80% of the area is in glass block.

Right: In the same period in which glass was being used to great dramatic effect in the entrance lobbies of their buildings in New York's Rockefeller Center, Harrison & Fouilhoux designed General Electric's WGY Broadcasting Station in Schenectady, New York, completed in 1938. The façade (*below*), functional but warm, combined the use of red brick and glass block with chromium.

Expressive of the tension, vigor, and energy of a new age, the curve became the most dynamic characteristic of the 1930s style. Found everywhere—in shop and showroom, hotel and public building—the curve suggested the streamline, hence modernity, to the American consumer.

Completed in 1936, Lurelle Guild's Alcoa Showroom in New York City (*above*), advertised aluminum not merely in the products displayed, but in the structure itself: lighting fixtures, furniture, and display stands were all built of aluminum. *Below*: Raymond Loewy's design for New York City's Cushman's was the model for similar bake shops in cities and towns throughout America.

The Cataract Hotel (*above*), in Sioux Falls, South Dakota, designed by Harold Spitznagel in 1937, featured a lavish use of curves in its lobby, particularly in the entrance to its restaurant and cocktail lounge.

Below: Designed in 1937, Reinhard Hofmeister's two branch offices of the Chase National Bank in Rockefeller Center were circular banking rooms, with terrazzo counters and platform rails running in an unbroken line, and circular domes overhead providing troughs for reflector lights.

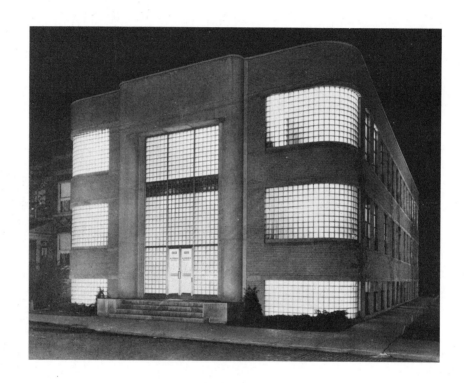

The Meyercord Company, a manufacturer of decalcomanias, opened its glass block office building in Chicago in 1938, decorating its interiors with its own products—notably in different patterns of Sans-Marb, an imitation marble so effective that only experts could tell that it was not real. Other applications of the company's products were suggested in decorative photomurals. All interiors and furnishings were designed by Abel Faidy; the building itself, by Julius Floto.

Three views of a combined living room—dining room—clients' reception room in Russel Wright's New York penthouse studio and apartment, 1934. The room was furnished entirely with special pieces, each experimental in character, and each serving multiple functions. Designed, in part, as a proving ground for furniture prior to commercial production, the studio illustrates Wright's principles of maximum flexibility of use.

Designed by Raymond Loewy and Lee Simonson for the 1934 Contemporary American Industrial Arts Exposition at New York's Metropolitan Museum of Art and planned to show that an office should be adapted to its function, this industrial designer's office and studio (*below*), intentionally resembles a clinic: a place where things are examined, studied, and diagnosed. It was constructed almost entirely of ivory formica and gunmetal.

Designed by Abel Faidy in 1936 for America's most innovative architectural photographers, the Hedrich-Blessing studio in Chicago featured a mirrored wall which doubled the apparent size of the reception room and reflected the photomural of the studio's work, then a radical decorative departure.

The private office (*opposite*), echoes the dramatic quality of the reception room. High and narrow, it emphasizes the proportions by a strip of photographs and by low, simple furniture. Because of its creative use of glass, the Hedrich-Blessing studio won the grand prize in the Pittsburgh Glass Institute competition of 1937.

A champion of good modern design, Henry Luce's Time Incorporated helped to popularize the idea of economic recovery through the creation of American functional objects, Luce's *Architectural Forum* remaining to this day the best pictorial record of excellent Depression Modern design. *Left:* Three views of Time Inc.'s conference room and reception areas, New York City, 1937.

In 1937, the architect William Lescaze designed rooms (*left and below*) for Time, featuring seating for interviews arranged in small sections and a receptionist's desk protected from cross-drafts by a glass screen tilted to avoid reflection.

Although only a small, local radio station, KSOO in Sioux Falls, South Dakota, required the same sound insulation needed by the large radio networks. In 1937, architect Harold Spitznagel, employing glass block and plate glass functionally and decoratively, produced the clean and efficient design pictured here.

The Sioux Falls architectural office that Spitznagel designed for himself in 1937 (*right*), featured what was probably the only glass block desk in America—and certainly the only one that was illuminated from within. Stark Venetian blinds on curtainless windows were already a cliché of modernism in America.

The Johnson Wax Administration Building—designed for the Racine, Wisconsin, company by Frank Lloyd Wright in 1937—is admittedly a work of architectural genius, but it is as well reflective of the period in which it was planned. Its flowing curves and horizontality identify it clearly as a work of the late '30s. From the floor of its large room for typists rise slender white concrete columns that taper from nine inches at the base to eighteen-foot disks at the ceiling. Between these circles falls natural light through patterned glass-tube skylights. Wright designed all the original furniture for the building, including the three-legged chairs, which tip over if the typist does not sit with correct posture.

Office furniture designed for Herman Miller, Inc., by Gilbert Rohde, 1936.

This almost casual-looking furniture (*below*), was designed in 1939 by Edward Durell Stone for the penthouse offices of Simon & Schuster, New York publishers. Stone, having created an all-glass office pavilion down the center of a building rooftop in Rockefeller Center, designed light furniture especially conducive to its setting.

The general trend of greater simplicity and directness is reflected in the variety and improved appearance of business machines in the 1930s. As the decade progressed, such machinery grew sleeker and more horizontal. The 1933 Dictaphone (*above, left*), although featuring for the first time a cover over the moving parts, revealed nevertheless a vertical bias. Six years later, re-designed by Raymond Loewy, the "Cameo" model (*above, right*) was ten pounds lighter and decidedly more horizontal.

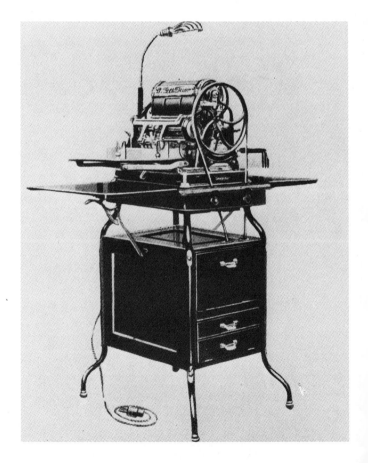

When, in 1933, Raymond Loewy re-designed the 1929 Gestetner duplicating machine (*below, left*), he created a functionally formed useful product (*below, right*), which was smoothly encased, its corners rounded off and its projections sheared away. The result was a new appearance of simplicity, efficiency, and attractiveness.

A late '30s model
of the Todd "Protectograph" check writer,
designed by Henry Dreyfuss.

Streamlined chromium pencil sharpener, designed by Raymond Loewy in 1934.

The 1935 model of the desk telephone set —designed by the engineering-design department of Bell Telephone Laboratories, with the assistance of an artist-consultant and an advisory committee of artists— was offered in a variety of finishes including ivory, gray, statuary bronze, oxidized silver, and in gold.

The Southern California Gas Co. commissioned E. C. and E. W. Taylor to design a display building that would emphasize the modernity of gas as a fuel as well as the appliances for sale. Gracefully curved, with well-organized lettering (silhouetted at night against lighted panels), the Hollywood structure opened in 1937.

Raymond Loewy's store front for Cushman's Bake Shop in New York (1937), and its hundreds of imitations across the nation, introduced countless Americans to their first taste of "the modern."

An early example (1934) of glass and stainless steel used to remodel (and "modernize") a restaurant in Canton, Ohio. Two years later, the "Modernize Main Street" movement began as a nationwide effort to improve the depressed economy.

Opened in 1940 in Taunton, Massachusetts, and standing in sharp relief against older structures, this five-and-dime, typical of scores of Woolworth stores built during the Depression, graphically illustrates the "Modernize Main Street" movement.

The building as billboard, a '30s innovation. The Star Electric Building, Newark, New Jersey (*opposite*), designed in 1936 by Barney Sumner Gruzen.

The lobby entrance of the Rockefeller Center showroom of the National Cash Register Company, designed in 1939 by Reinhard & Hofmeister and handsomely arranged for display.

Model of rotary filling station, designed in 1934 by Raymond Loewy. As the motorist's car was driven onto the turntable, his car was serviced within two minutes with gasoline, oil, water, and air. Two of these red-white-and-blue porcelained-steel service stations were built in New York City.

The elevator bank and men's shoe department of the Wm. H. Block Co., Indianapolis, Indiana (*opposite, top*), modernized by Vonnegut, Bohn and Mueller, and Pereira and Pereira in 1934.

An unusual use of glass for the side walls of an escalator (*opposite, below*), designed in 1936 by Eleanor LeMaire for The Emporium, San Francisco, California.

John Vassos' Coca-Cola dispenser, 1933. Egmont Arens's A & P coffee packaging, 1934. Russel Wright's vending machine, 1934. Raymond Loewy's Elizabeth Arden cosmetics packaging, c. 1936.

Styled in 1937 for aviatrix-cosmetician Jacqueline Cochran and incorporating the motifs of sky-writing and revolving airplane propellers in the design, Raymond Loewy's "Wings to Beauty" cosmetics packaging (*opposite*), appealed to "contemporary-minded women" in a day before *Fear of Flying*.

Although the Depression world of streamlined transportation boasted the names of such prominent designers as Norman Bel Geddes, Henry Dreyfuss, and Otto Kuhler, Raymond Loewy's was the one best known to the American public. These visualizations of the future were executed by Loewy in 1938 as part of the exhibit on transportation at the New York World's Fair the following year. Included are a four-decker airplane, streamlined train, triple-unit truck, streamlined automobile, double-decker autobus, autotaxi, and single-masted ocean liner.

M ost famous of the streamlined trains of the early '30s, the Burlington Zephyr (*above*), built by the Budd Manufacturing Company, captured the imagination of a speed-conscious America when it was first exhibited at Chicago's Century of Progress Exposition in 1934. An invitation to display it on the streets of Philadelphia, in front of the Art Alliance's Dynamic Design exhibit, was rejected the same year.

R aymond Loewy aboard his K4S streamlined locomotive (*opposite*), built for the Pennsylvania Railroad in 1936.

Raymond Loewy's "The Eagle" (above, left), a six-car, air-conditioned, streamlined train designed for the Missouri Pacific Railroad in 1938. The GG-1 electrical locomotive (above, right), the first butt-welded engine in the United States, designed with engineers of the Pennsylvania Railroad by Loewy in 1936.

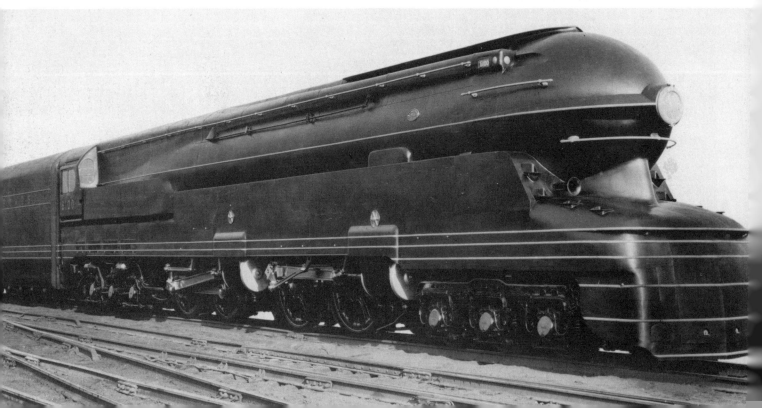

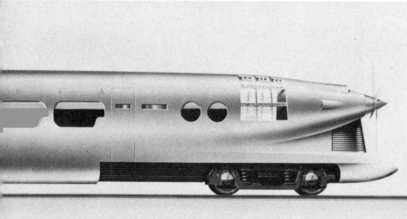

Never built, this experimental single-unit fast-motorized commuter train (*opposite*), was designed by Loewy for the Pennsylvania Railroad in 1932. *Below*: The S-1 (*left*), designed by Loewy in collaboration with the Pennsylvania Railroad in 1937, was in its day the world's largest high-speed locomotive. Loewy's K4S (*right*), built in 1936.

The interiors of Raymond Loewy's trains reflected his belief that they should equal the standard of the modern home. *Above:* The curved interior of The Eagle's observation car, 1938. *Left:* Bar-lounge car, The Broadway Limited, 1936. Contemporary advertisements spoke of this car as "an intimate and smart club on wheels. Curved wall sections, murals, upholstered banquettes, rich carpeting, and 'sunbeam' mirrors lend distinction to travel and entertainment by rail."

Loewy's bar-lounge car, The General (*right*), 1936. Walls: gray harewood Flexwood. Ceiling: alcove, gold leaf; lower deck, rust. Floor covering: mauve taupe carpet. Chairs: rust, and natural-colored leather. Sofas: natural-colored leather. Tables: gray Micarta. Venetian blinds: gray paint. Bar counter: mahogany. Bar: redwood burl Flexwood, bronze opalescent trim. Mirror: flesh-tinted.

All concrete curves and buttresses, the World's Fair Station of the Long Island Railroad, 1939 (*opposite, top*), was pictured in the Fair's *Official Guide Book* in this manner: "The slogan of the Pennsylvania Railroad, 'From the World of Today to the World of Tomorrow in ten minutes for ten cents,' describes the service of the Long Island Railroad which brings you swiftly to the Fair from Pennsylvania Terminal in Manhattan. Twelve-car shuttle trains operate on a two-minute headway. The Long Island's World's Fair Station has a capacity of 20,000 persons an hour."

Ticket office, Burlington Railroad, Denver, Colorado, 1938 (*opposite, bottom*). The sweeping curves of the gleaming chromium-steel counter and the recessed fluorescent lighting were intended by architects Holabird & Root to suggest the lines of the Burlington's own famous streamliners.

The Douglas DC-3 (*right*), 1937. The most successful Depression civil airliner illustrates the ovoid gliding form and smooth, continuous surface of streamlining. Earning its nickname of "workhorse," the DC-3 eventually carried more than half a billion passengers over the years, not counting millions of servicemen during World War II.

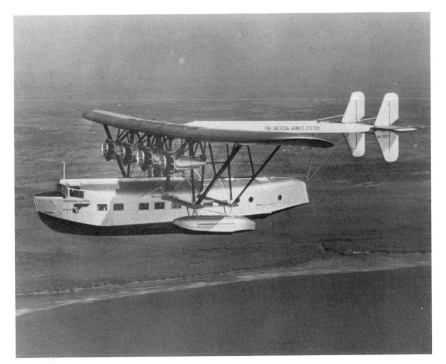

The first Flying Clipper (*left*), 1931. Flagship of the most famous airplanes of the decade, the Sikorsky S-40 captured the imagination of the nation when, in 1933, a brace of dancing chorus girls, led by Ginger Rogers, went *Flying Down to Rio* aboard its glistening wings. *Below:* The Dixie Clipper, last of Pan American Airways' Flying Clippers, 1939.

Brochure advertising TWA's Stratoliner, designed by Raymond Loewy, 1939.

Beauty and Convenience

CHARM
ROOM

This Charm Room for the ladies represents styl-
ing and design as advanced as the TWA
Stratoliner itself. A masterpiece in convenient
arrangement, the room has full view lighted
mirrors, two smartly styled dressing tables, upholstered seats, wash basin with hot and cold
water, built-in towel shelves, ash trays, and
handy waste containers. Mirrors are lighted by
modern tube fixtures, while the entire room is
softly illuminated by indirect lighting.

Interior, Dixie Clipper, 1939.

Interior, Douglas DC-3, 1939.

...BINED IN BOEING STRATOLINER APPOINTMENTS

MEN'S
LOUNGE

Here the tallest man can stand erect with headroom to spare. And all fixtures have been placed at customary home levels . . . including the tube-lighted plate glass mirrors . . . including the tube-lighted your shaving "stance!" ℂ From conveniently placed towels to handy outlets for electric razors, every detail of this cleverly designed lounge has been carefully studied with one purpose in view . . . to make the process of freshening up aloft both easy and pleasant.

The TWA TRANSCONTINENTAL Airline

The *Princess Anne*, a Chesapeake Bay commuters' steamer, designed by Raymond Loewy in 1933 and launched in 1936, was the nearest approach to streamlining to appear on the Atlantic seaboard until Loewy's luxury liner, the *S. S. Panama*, made its maiden voyage in 1938. *Far left:* The Main Salon of the *S. S. Panama*, the first ocean liner decorated in the simple, restrained, contemporary American style. *Above and left:* the streamlined *Princess Anne.*

Although most people think of the Studebaker as an innovative automobile of the
late 1940s, it was already a trend-setter in the
'30s. *Center:* The 1938 Studebaker President,
selected by the American Federation of Arts
as the "best looking car of the year," an un-
precedented award. *Left:* 1939 Studebaker and
S-1 locomotive with their designer, Raymond
Loewy. *Right:* 1938 Studebaker Champion cruis-
ing sedan.

Because of the commercial success of Chrysler's Airflow in 1934, all Detroit turned to streamlining as automobiles became lower and more horizontal. *Counterclockwise, from left to right:* 1937 Lincoln Zephyr V-12, 1936 Cord, 1936 Plymouth sedan, 1937 Mercury, and 1938 Lincoln Zephyr. The justly famous, but short-lived Cord was America's most advanced front-engined automobile during the Depression.

The '30s was a decade of massive construction: public buildings, dams, highways—and, especially, bridges. Above, two of the finest: The Bronx-Whitestone Bridge, 1939 (*left*) and The Triborough, 1936 (*right*), both designed for New York's Triborough Bridge Authority by O. H. Ammann, Allston Dana, and Aymar Embury.

City offices, the police department, city jail, water department, rifle facilities, and assembly hall were included in Harold Spitznagel's design for the compact Municipal Building in Sioux Falls, South Dakota, completed in 1937. Executed in brick, with granite base and entrance, it expresses the Depression's rejection of superfluous decoration and waste space. The interiors, of flush wood panels or plaster, reflect the conservative, unpretentious exterior. The frescoes in the Commissions' room were painted by Edwin Boyd Johnson.

Although most American public buildings continued to imitate classical models, an increasing number turned to the contemporary Depression Modern style. *Opposite, from top to bottom:* Alpena County Courthouse, Alpena, Michigan, William H. Kuni, architect, 1935. Ector County Courthouse, Odessa, Texas, Elmer Withers, architect, 1938. State Capitol, Bismarck, North Dakota, Holabird & Root, architects, 1934. *Above:* State Capitol, Salem, Oregon, Trowbridge & Livingston and Francis Keally, associated architects, 1938.

During the Depression, the WPA constructed local post offices that were exceeded in ugliness only by those built today. One of the few exceptions, the U.S. Post Office at Miami Beach, Florida (*below*), opened in 1939. *Opposite* (*above*): The Houston (Texas) Building & Loan Association offices, John F. Staub and Kenneth Franzheim, architects, 1938. *Opposite* (*below*): Bronxville (New York) Federal Savings and Loan Association building, George F. Root III and Frederick J. Hartwig, architects, 1939.

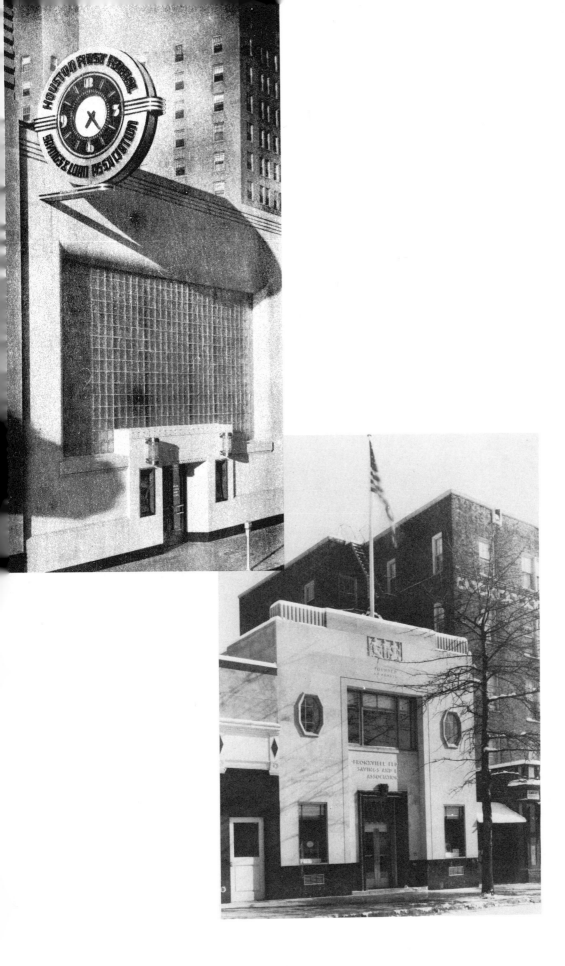

Few public buildings of the '30s more dramatically demonstrated the trend of horizontality than did schools, several of which were worlds apart from the vertical blocks of the previous decade. *Left to right:* Edward L. Bailey Junior High School, Jackson, Mississippi, N. W. Overstreet and A. H. Town, architects, 1937. Cranbrook Institute of Sciences Building, Bloomfield Hills, Michigan, Eliel Saarinen, architect, 1938. Columbia High School, Columbia, Mississippi, N. W. Overstreet and A. H. Town, architects, 1937.

Museums, too, surrendered their traditional eclecticism and became increasingly modern, the decade culminating in Edward Durell Stone and Philip Goodwin's magnificent Museum of Modern Art, New York City, 1939 (*opposite*). *Right* (*above*): The nation's first modern museum structure, the Avery Memorial of the Wadsworth Atheneum, Hartford, Connecticut, Morris & O'Connor, architects, 1934. *Right* (*below*): Fine Arts Center, Colorado Springs, Colorado, John Gaw Meem, architect, 1936.

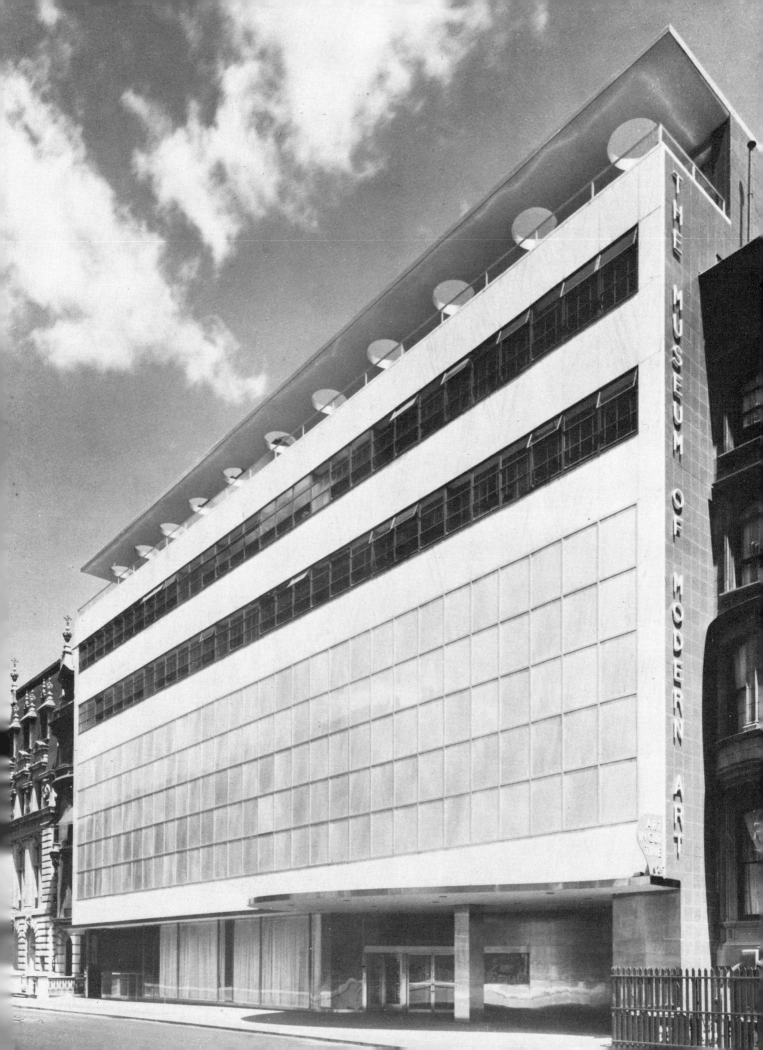

Walter Dorwin Teague's lounge for the Ford Exhibit, New York World's Fair, 1939.

Trans-Lux Theater, New York City, Thomas W. Lamb, architect, 1938.

Hollywood Theater (*right*), Sioux Falls, South Dakota, Harold Spitznagel, architect, 1937.

Savar Theater, Camden, New Jersey, 1936.

In these streamlined, reclining movie theater seats (*opposite*), Depression youth emulated Ruby Keeler and Dick Powell "Pettin' in the Park." The smart aisle light reveals the cult of the unholy trinity. *Above:* Elegantly curved and unornamented, the '30s movie theater bore little resemblance to the rococo motion picture palaces of the previous decade. One of the most handsome Depression Modern theaters was Chicago's Esquire, designed by Pereira and Pereira and opened in 1937.

International Casino, New York City, 1937. Ingeniously designed by Donald Deskey to by-pass the local law limiting the number of bars in an establishment to one, this multi-leveled nightclub featured a spectacular "spiral" bar that served customers along the complete length of stairs. The casino boasted the first escalator in a place of public entertainment.

Ladies' Lounge, Hollywood Theater, Sioux Falls, South Dakota, Harold Spitznagel, designer, 1937.

B uilt in Mt. Kisco, New York, and completed in 1935, two years after it was designed, the house of Richard H. Mandel was a collaboration between architect Edward Durell Stone and designer Donald Deskey, functioning as "interior architect"—with the assistance of the owner, who was an associate of Deskey.

T he exterior (*above*) illustrates the new horizontality, corners broken only by one flowing curve where a rounded glass block bay is introduced. Deskey's interiors (*opposite*), colorful and warm, but reinforcing the functionalism of the exterior, succeeded in bringing indoors the spaciousness of the new horizontality.

So intense was reaction to the Ulrich Kowalski house (*opposite and above*), designed in 1934 by Edward Durell Stone, that zoning ordinances in Mt. Kisco, New York, were modified to prevent "further desecration of the community."

Architectural model of the house of Mrs. Charles I. Liebman, Mt. Kisco, New York, designed in 1937 by Stone but never built.

Writing of his career, which has extended over fifty years, one of the great American architects, George Fred
Keck, writes that architects "build at a given time, using all the devices, ideas, and materials and needs of *that*
time, and what comes out is the result of such thinking." What came out of his assimilation of ideas current in the
Depression was one of the best houses of the '30s: the Herbert Bruning residence in Wilmette, Illinois, designed in 1936.

The Herbert Bruning residence, 1936
(*above and following page*).

Living room, decorated by Gladys Freeman, in one of four guest houses, all designed by Edward Durell Stone, on Mepkin Plantation, Moncks Corners, South Carolina, winter home of Henry R. Luce, 1937.

Detail of living room, Albert C. Koch residence, Cambridge, Massachusetts, Edward Durell Stone, architect, 1936.

The most extraordinary house in Depression America was undoubtedly the residence (*above*) that Earl Butler built in Des Moines, Iowa, between 1935 and 1937. Working in close collaboration with his architects, Kraetsch and Kraetsch, Butler constructed a fire, tornado, earthquake, and termite-proof residence, permitting no conventional decoration since he believed that "simplicity and good design are much more restful and inherently beautiful in a home." Among the special features were an unusual central ramp, air conditioning, dishwasher and disposal, an electric eye to open and close garage doors, a small storage room for freezing game, an extra ice-cube freezer with a 675-cube capacity, and an intercommunicating telephone system.

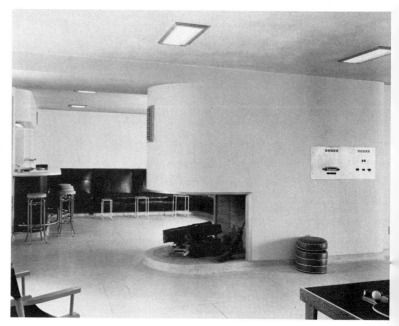

Above: Central ramp. *Far left:* Basement recreation room. *Left:* Study.

The crescent-shaped residence in Lake Forest, Illinois, that George Fred Keck designed for B. J. Cahn in 1937. Having seen Keck's "House of Tomorrow" at the Century of Progress, Mrs. Cahn requested that he build "the house of the day after tomorrow." What Keck designed was one of the most beautiful houses in America, whether seen by day (*above*) or at night (*left*).

Right (*above*):
High-ceilinged living room, rugless and curtainless for ease in maintenance.
Right (*below*):
Bedroom with built-in beds.

Five views of the Frank Altschul Library, Stamford, Connecticut, designed in 1939 by Edward Durell Stone. A private retreat, planned for a publisher of limited editions and situated on a large estate, the structure featured sliding glass walls, then a novel architectural innovation. The interiors were designed by Virginia Connor.

Collier's House of Ideas (*opposite, above, and right*), an exhibit built in 1940 by Edward Durell Stone on a terrace in Rockefeller Center, introduced the use of redwood to the East. The furniture was designed by Jens Risom and Dan Cooper.

Harrison and Fouilhoux's *Ladies' Home Journal* House (*left*), built for the 1937 New York Home Show, featured a rounded glass wall which, at the push of a button, disappeared into the ground, admitting the garden indoors.

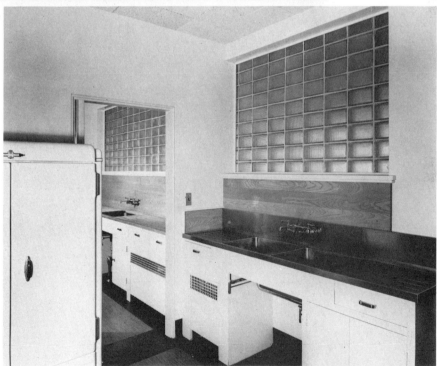

Completed in 1937, this dignified residence of steel, brick, and glass, built for Henry B. Robertson in Centerville, Delaware, was designed by Victorine and Samuel Homsey. Its interiors repeat the essentially simple forms of the exterior, the integration of design and decoration heightened by the almost complete absence of ornamentation.

The house of Alvin Greif (*above and opposite*), on Rivo Alta Island, Florida, designed by T. Trip Russell and Igor Polevitzky, and completed in 1938.

A striking transformation of a 19th-century brownstone in New York City by William Lescaze, designed for his own use and employing glass block several years before it was a popular building material, 1934.

A similar, and even more dramatic transformation of a 19th-century Chicago row house by James F. Eppenstein, 1939.

As modern today as the day it was built, this Chicago apartment house (*above*) was designed by George Fred Keck in 1937. (The photograph was taken in May 1975.)

Certainly the most beautiful apartment house constructed in New York during the 1930s, The Rockefeller Apartments (*opposite*), designed by J. André Fouilhoux and Wallace K. Harrison in 1936, clearly demonstrates the Depression Modern style: an unadorned façade and graceful curves.

The 1930s' love of the curve is everywhere evident in this Milwaukee apartment house, designed by Herbert W. Tullgren and completed in 1939—from the building's graceful bays and its circular driveway *(left)* to the entrance foyer of a typical apartment *(below)* and a hallway corridor leading to the lobby *(opposite)*.

Furniture designed by Russel Wright. *Opposite, above:* "American Modern" dining room, 1935. *Opposite, below:* "Blonde" maple "American Modern" living room with contemporary Morris chairs, each with adjustable back, 1936. *Above:* Upholstered sectional furniture designed for Heywood-Wakefield, 1933.

Furniture designed for Herman Miller, Inc., by Gilbert Rohde. *Opposite, above:* Laurel wood drop-front desk, c. 1936. *Below:* Corner of a living room, featuring radio end table, 1936. *Opposite, below:* Bentwood side chair and glass-top table with brush-chromium support, 1934.

 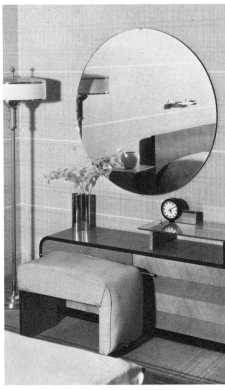

Two views of a bedroom designed by Gilbert Rohde for Herman Miller, Inc., 1934.

Black lacquer and chrome bedroom suite designed by Norman Bel Geddes for the Simmons Co., displayed in the window of Carson Pirie Scott during the second year of Chicago's Century of Progress Exposition, 1934.

Grand piano (*opposite, above*) designed by Walter Dorwin Teague for Steinway & Sons, 1939. Grand piano (*opposite, below*) designed by Russel Wright for Wurlitzer, c. 1932.

Detail of living room (*below*) decorated by John D. Gerald for B. Altman's "Modern House," New York City, 1937.

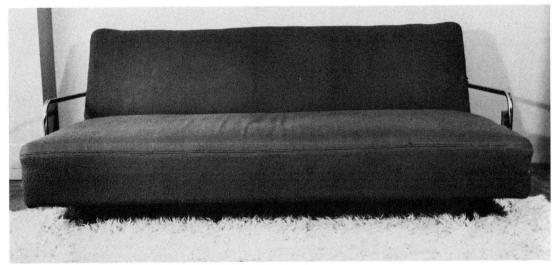

Sculptor, architect, designer, poet, visionary, Frederick Kiesler was a genius the majority of whose works are out of place in a volume dedicated to the mundane. But even Kiesler's furniture of the '30s was touched by the spirit of the times: the urge to simplify, to strip bare is everywhere apparent.

Far left, above: One of a nest of cast aluminum coffee tables, 1936. *Far left, below:* Aluminum kidney-shaped tables, 1938. *Center:* Bookcase with adjustable sycamore shelves and chrome supports, 1935. *Above, top:* Chrome couch/sofa/bed, originally covered with white leather and an excellent example of Kiesler's concept of multiple use of furniture, 1935. *Above:* Chrome ash tray, 1935.

"Modern Blue Kitchen," a model room designed to display the latest pattern of linoleum by the Armstrong Cork Company, 1936.

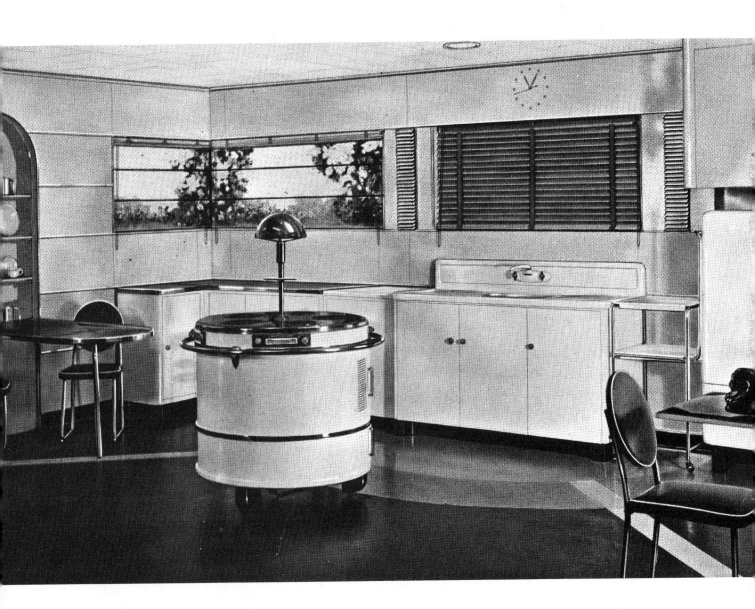

"The Kitchen of Tomorrow," as envisioned by the Briggs Manufacturing Company, 1935. The cylindrical structure in the foreground is an electric range.

Bathrooms designed in 1940 (*opposite*) and in 1938 (*above*) by Edward Durell Stone. The Leda and the Swan chair and mural reflect either the influence of the famous Surrealism exhibition of 1936 or a droll sense of humor; perhaps both.

Plumbing hardware (*below*), designed in 1932 by George Sakier.

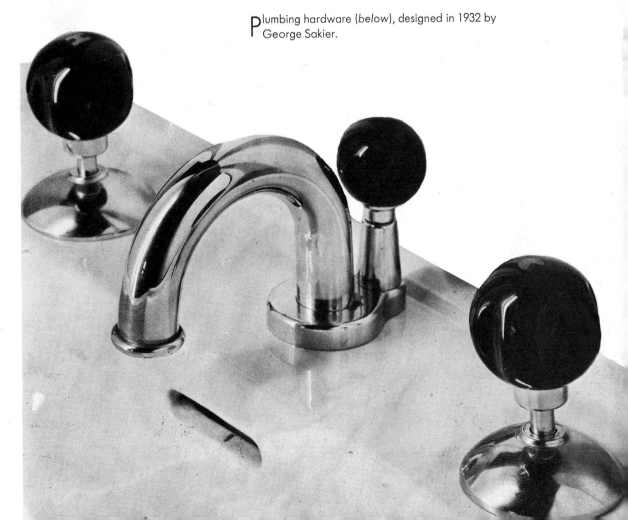

Designs by Russel Wright. Smoking set *(opposite, above)*, chrome, cork, wood, and glass, 1933. Aquarium *(below)*, chromium and glass, 1933. Bookend *(above)*, c. 1930.

Home accessories by Russel Wright. Handmade silver flatware (*opposite*), c. 1930. Ice bucket and tongs (*above*), 1933. Spun aluminum stove-to-table wear (*center*), 1933. Bun warmer (*right*), c. 1933.

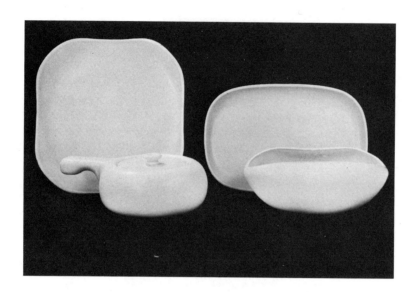

Russel Wright's "American Modern" dinnerware (1937) was in its time immensely popular, favored in particular by young couples starting married life in the final years of the Depression. Its graceful, flowing lines owe as much to the influence of Surrealism's amorphous shapes as to Wright's desire to break away from the geometric forms of the early '30s.

In 1934 Lurelle Guild designed a line of aluminum utensils for Wear-Ever that were so forward-looking for their day that they were displayed in the Philadelphia Art Alliance's Dynamic Design show. *Opposite*: Whistling tea kettle with Bakelite handle and knob (*above*). Contrast (*below*) between old-style tea kettle and Guild's streamline model. *Above*: Guild's 1934 adaptation of an early American coffeepot.

Designs by Lurelle Guild for the International Silver Company, 1934, the first time in the company's history in which signed pieces were offered. *Opposite:* The Glory Bowl (*below*) and The Bordeaux Dish (*above*). *Above:* Regency Covered Dish (*top*), The Empire Bowl (*center*), and The Brompton Wine Cooler (*right*).

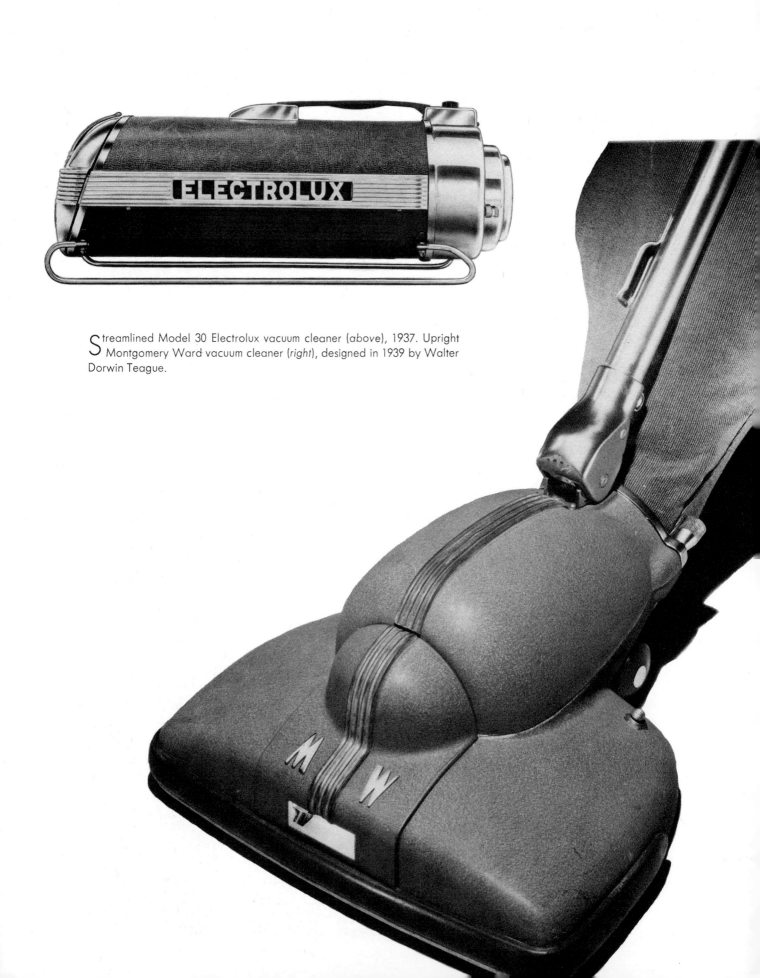

Streamlined Model 30 Electrolux vacuum cleaner (*above*), 1937. Upright Montgomery Ward vacuum cleaner (*right*), designed in 1939 by Walter Dorwin Teague.

G eneral Electric mixer (*left*), designed in 1934 by Lurelle Guild.
G Coldspot refrigerator (*below*) by Raymond Loewy, 1938.

A Depression ideal: creating inexpensive, well-designed objects for the common man. Mass-produced glassware (*opposite and above*), designed for the Fostoria Company by George Sakier, c. 1934.

Depression Modern Steuben glass was probably the best-designed American glass since that produced in the 18th century. *Above:* Table Glass, designed by Frederick Carder, 1934. *Opposite:* Ring Stopper Decanter, 1934.

Unlike the more elaborate and ornate pieces produced before and since, Steuben glass created during the Depression was either starkly plain or simply etched. In the opinion of many, the unadorned pieces are among the most stunningly beautiful designs of the decade. *Above:* Bowl with solid crimped base, designed by Walter Heintze, 1938. *Center:* Mariner's Bowl, designed by Sidney Waugh, 1935. *Opposite, above:* Gazelle Bowl, designed by Sidney Waugh, 1935. *Opposite, below:* Teardrop Candlesticks, designed by F. B. Sellew, 1937.

This 1939 RCA-Victor console cost $450 and was America's first popular-priced television receiver. Its cabinet, bulky and clumsy, displayed the curves favored by contemporary consumers.

The first table model radio and the first practical portable radio (*opposite, inset*), designed by Russel Wright for Wurlitzer, c. 1933. RCA-Victor radio-phonograph (*below*), featuring controls inspired by aeronautics, 1935.

Wallace K. Harrison and J. André Fouilhoux's Trylon and Perisphere, 1939. The symbol of the New York World's Fair represented the final distillation of more than one thousand preliminary sketches—the use of the sphere and triangle (geometry's simplest and most fundamental forms) resulting from a determination to strike a new note in design, yet one simple in form and structurally sound. A streamlined phoenix emerging triumphant from the devastation of the Great Depression—the very essence of the Depression Modern style.

CREDITS

In this list of photographic credits, the following abbreviations are used: a (above), b (below), c (center), l (left), and r (right).

Jacket: Edward Durell Stone Associates, an Ezra Stoller photograph. *Frontispiece:* Republic Steel Corporation.

Preface: p. 17 (counterclockwise, l. to r.), Dunbar Furniture, Pan American World Airways, Halle's, Raymond Loewy International, Inc.

Depression Modern: An Appreciation: Evolutionary charts, Raymond Loewy International, Inc.; p. 24, author; p. 25, New York Public Library Picture Collection; p. 29, Republic Steel Corporation; p. 31, The Austin Company; p. 35, Raymond Loewy International, Inc.; p. 44, Russel Wright.

The Thirties Style in America: An Album: pp. 50-51, The Austin Company; p. 52, The Hecht Company (a), The Campana Corporation (c); p. 53, The Austin Company; p. 54, Johnson & Johnson (a), Arizona Historical Society (c), U. S. Forest Products Laboratory (b); p. 55, *Shreveport Times,* a Langston McEachern photograph (a), Hedrich-Blessing (b); p. 56, The Austin Company; p. 57, CBS; p. 58, Steuben Glass (a), Wallace K. Harrison (b); p. 59, Wallace K. Harrison.

P. 60, Aluminum Company of America (a), Raymond Loewy International, Inc. (b); p. 61, Northwest Architectural Archives (a), The Chase Manhattan Bank (b); pp. 62-63, The Meyercord Company, Hedrich-Blessing photographs; p. 64, Russel Wright; p. 65, Russel Wright (a), Raymond Loewy International, Inc. (b); pp. 66-67, Hedrich-Blessing; pp. 68-69, Time Incorporated.

Pp. 70-71, Northwest Architectural Archives; pp. 72-73, Johnson Wax photographs; p. 74, Herman Miller, Inc., p. 75, Edward Durell Stone Associates; pp. 76-77, Dictaphone Corporation (a), Raymond Loewy International, Inc. (b); p. 78, Burroughs Corporation, Business Forms and Supplies Group; p. 79, Raymond Loewy International, Inc. (a), A. T. & T. (b).

P. 80, Southern California Gas Company (a), Raymond Loewy International, Inc. (b); p. 81, Republic Steel Corporation (a), F. W. Woolworth Co. (b); p. 82, Star Electrical Supply Co.; p. 83, NCR Corporation; p. 84, Raymond Loewy International, Inc.; p. 85, Wm. H. Block Co. (a), The Emporium (b); p. 86, The Archives, The Coca-Cola Company (a.l.), The Great Atlantic and Pacific Tea Company (a.c.), Russel Wright (a.r.), Raymond Loewy International, Inc. (b); pp. 87-89, Raymond Loewy International, Inc.

P. 90, Republic Steel Corporation; pp. 91-96 (a), Raymond Loewy International, Inc.; p. 96 (b), Hedrich-Blessing; pp. 98-99, Pan American World Airways.

P. 100, author (a), Pan American World Airways (b); p. 101, Pan American World Airways; pp. 102-5, Raymond Loewy International, Inc.; pp. 106-7, New York Public Library Picture Collection; p. 108, Triborough Bridge & Tunnel Authority, a Richard Averill Smith photograph; p. 109, The Museum of the City of New York, a Berenice Abbott photograph.

Pp. 110-11, The Spitznagel Partners; p. 112, Alpena County Clerk (a), Ector County Clerk (c), Holabird & Root (b); p. 113, Oregon State Highway Division; p. 114, E. H. Daws; p. 115, Houston First Savings (a), First Federal Savings and Loan Association of New York (b); pp. 116-17, A. L. McCormick (a), Cranbrook Educational Community (c), Columbia

Public Schools (b); p. 118, Wadsworth Atheneum (a), Colorado Springs Fine Arts Center (b); p. 119, Edward Durell Stone Associates.

Pp. 120-21, Walter Dorwin Teague Associates, Inc., Robert Damora photographs; pp. 122-23, Trans-Lux (a), Northwest Architectural Archives (c), Republic Steel Corporation (b); 124-25, Hedrich-Blessing; p. 126, Donald Deskey; p. 127, Northwest Architectural Archives; pp. 128-29, Edward Durell Stone Associates.

Pp. 130-31, Edward Durell Stone Associates, Ezra Stoller photographs (l. and r.a.), a Louis Checkman photograph (r.b.); pp. 132-34, George Fred Keck, Hedrich-Blessing photographs; p. 135, Edward Durell Stone Associates, a Gottscho-Schleisner photograph (a), an Ezra Stoller photograph (b); pp. 136-37, Hedrich-Blessing; pp. 138-39, George Fred Keck, Hedrich-Blessing photographs.

Pp. 140-43 (a, c), Edward Durell Stone Associates, Ezra Stoller photographs; p. 143 (b), Wallace K. Harrison; pp. 144-145, Robert Damora; pp. 146-47, T. Trip Russell; p. 148, The Museum of the City of New York; p. 149, Hedrich-Blessing.

P. 150, Wallace K. Harrison; p. 151-53, Hedrich-Blessing; pp. 154-55, Russel Wright; pp. 156-58, Herman Miller, Inc.; p. 159, Simmons Company.

P. 160, Walter Dorwin Teague Associates, Inc. (a), Russel Wright (b); p. 161, B. Altman & Co.; pp. 162-63, Lillian Kiesler, Lenny Di Caro photographs; p. 164, Armstrong Cork Company; p. 165, author; pp. 166-67 (a), Edward Durell Stone Associates, Ezra Stoller photographs; p. 167 (b), George Sakier; pp. 168-69, Russel Wright.

Pp. 170-73, Russel Wright; pp. 174-75, Wear-Ever Aluminum, Inc.; pp. 176-77, author; p. 178, Electrolux Corporation (a), Walter Dorwin Teague Associates, Inc. (b); p. 179, author (a), Raymond Loewy International, Inc. (b).

Pp. 180-81, George Sakier; pp. 182-85, Steuben Glass; p. 186, RCA (a), Russel Wright (b); p. 187, RCA; p. 188, Wallace K. Harrison.

I N D E X